FAMOUS AMERICAN
CHURCHES AND SHRINES

CATHOLIC EDITION

Walter T. Murphy, *Editor*

WALMUR PUBLISHING COMPANY
Bloomfield Hills, Michigan

Printed in the United States of America

BASILICA OF OUR LADY of Perpetual Help, Boston Massachusetts.

ENGRAVED BRONZE DOORS leading to the Blessed Sacrament Chapel behind the main altar at the National Shrine of Our Lady of the Snows, Belleville, Illinois.

MISSION DOLORES, and Basilica, San Francisco, California.

HIGH ALTAR of the Basilica of St. Adalbert, Buffalo, New York.

OUR LADY OF CZESTOCHOWA Shrine, Garfield Heights, Ohio.

TABLE OF CONTENTS

THE MISSION OF SAN ANTONIO de Isleta at Isleta pueblo south of Albuquerque, New Mexico. During the rebellion of 1680 the old church was burned and the Indians used its blackened walls as a corral.

INTRODUCTION

Few of the thousands of Americans who visit Europe's religious attractions—Cathedrals, Shrines, religious centers—ever get around to seeing famous churches and religious attractions in the United States.

One reason for the popularity of Europe's churches and shrines is that guidebooks and other promotional literature are available on virtually every European newsstand. Not so, however, for America's famous churches and shrines, for which no popular guidebook is available.

The fact remains that churches of magnificent architecture, churches with significant historic and cultural tradition, churches with paintings, mosaics and other great art, are plentiful in the United States. In addition, there are scores of religious "attractions" that are rewarding for the tourist seeking something different, something exciting.

In this era of ecumenism, this guidebook, admittedly selective, may be helpful, perhaps even stimulating, to people of all faiths. It is noted that doors to these churches and shrines are open every day, including Sunday. A visit can be a meaningful experience.

We express our thanks to the many priests and other religious editors of Catholic and secular publications, and directors of Catholic Information Centers who have aided in the selection of material and photographs. More specifically, our thanks to the following:

Susanne C. Slye, National Council of Catholic Men, Washington, D.C.; **James F. Irmiter,** New World Travel Service, Chicago; **William Fugazy,** Fugazy Travel, New York City; **William Ladyka,** Michigan Catholic, Detroit; **W. F. Blakeslee, C.S.P.,** Mobile, Ala.; **Sister Fulgentia Joseph, C.S.J.,** Freedoms Foundation, Valley Forge, Penn.; **Miss Lucy Boka,** Catholic Information Center, St. Louis, Mo.; **Rt. Rev. Msgr. Charles W. Popell,** St. Andrews' Cathedral, Grand Rapids, Mich.; **Rev. Lambert Gattman, O.S.B.,** Ave Maria Grotto, St. Bernard, Ala.; **Miss Esther Millman,** Friends of Old St. Ferdinand, Inc., Florissant, Mo.; **Edward Lalley,** The Globe, Sioux City, Iowa; **Rev. Raymond E. Whelan,** The Advance Register, Wichita, Kansas; **Rev. Shamus M. Loftus, O.F.N. Conv.,** Catholic Information Center, Binghamton, N.Y.; **Very Rev. Francis A. Quinn,** The Monitor, San Francisco, Calif.; **Rev. Donnan Herbe, O.F.M.,** St. Michael's, Arizona; **Mrs. Elaine Driscoll,** Catholic Information Center, Hartford, Conn.; **Catherine E. McMullen,** Milwaukee, Wis.; **Hilda Murphy,** Dearborn, Michigan; **Very Rev. J. P. Sammon, O.M.I.,** San Antonio, Texas; **His Eminence, Francis Cardinal Spellman.**

April 1, 1968   W. T. M.

4

FAMOUS AMERICAN

CHURCHES

AND

SHRINES

THE ABBEY CHURCH of Conception Abbey, Conception, Missouri, was started in 1882 as the center of the Monastery's liturgical life. Pope Pius XII raised the church to the rank of Minor Basilica on September 14, 1940.

NINETEEN CHURCHES
IN THE UNITED STATES
RAISED TO ROYAL RANK
OF MINOR BASILICA

BASILICAN PAVILION

Most Americans know of the great basilicas of Rome—St. John Lateran, St. Peter's, St. Paul's outside the Walls, and St. Mary Major.

Relatively few, however, are aware that various Holy Fathers have elevated nineteen U.S. churches to the royal rank of Minor Basilica.

The term Basilica denotes a distinguished church upon which either ancient custom or papal decree has bestowed the name as a title of extreme honor.

A Basilica is also known popularly as the Pope's home away from home. Two symbols distinguish a church as a Basilica: the Basilican canopeum or umbrella, and a tintinnabulum, a small bell mounted upon an elaborate frame and pole.

The canopeum is a large symbolic umbrella made of twelve long strips of cloth alternating in red and yellow. It is used traditionally to protect the Holy Father when he goes from one Basilica to another; in the Church, it is always half-open for instant use. Fully open, it is 14 feet across. The 12-foot stem of the umbrella is the carrying pole topped with an orb and a cross.

The tintinnabulum is six feet high, carved of wood is an elaborate style and generally ornamented with gold leaf. The bell itself is not more than six inches at the mouth and is rung only when carried in procession. The frame for the bell is crowned with a carved papal tiara and keys.

The right to those two insignia is a pontifical concession for all time.

9

BASILICAS

ALABAMA

The Basilica of the Immaculate Conception was born of a twenty-by-fifty foot log cabin, built in 1828, and described at that time as a "poor wooden barn, destitute of any kind of ornament." The present magnificent Cathedral-Basilica, marked by its classic portico facing Claiborne street, is an outstanding landmark of downtown Mobile. Majestic twin towers were erected around 1890, and subsequently, imported stained glass windows were added. Early in the morning of March 19, 1954, a fire completely destroyed the sanctuary. During the reconstruction, the damaged stained glass windows were dismantled and shipped to Munich, Germany, where the company that had installed them was able to make restorations from the original cartoons in their files. March 10, 1962, the Cathedral was elevated to the rank of Minor Basilica.

CALIFORNIA

California has two basilicas, both intimately associated with the famed California mission chain established by Father Junipero Serra, foremost of the Franciscan missionaries.

Mission San Carlos Borromeo, number two in the mission chain, was raised to a Basilica February 5, 1960. Located near Carmel, this Mission is one of the major historical landmarks in California. Many reminders of the early years of its founding (1770) are displayed, including Indian carvings, home and farming implements, clothing. The remains of Father Junipero are buried at the altar of a church adjacent to the mission which is still undergoing restoration.

* * *

Mission Dolores Basilica, 3321 61st St., San Francisco, is the beautiful parish church adjoining Mission San Francisco de Assis, popularly known as Dolores. The Mission was the sixth established under Father Serra, in 1776. The Mission's walls are four feet thick, the roof has the original timbers and tiles. The timbers are rough hewn redwood lashed together with rawhide. The Basilica was opened on Christmas Day, 1918, and contains numerous art treasures. Among them are the stained glass windows which represent the twenty-one missions of California; medallions around the nave with pictures of the twelve Apostles: and mosiacs of Fathers Francisco Palou and Junipero Serra. Mission Dolores Basilica was elevated to Basilican rank February 8, 1952.

ILLINOIS

Chicago's famed Our Lady of Sorrows on Jackson Boulevard was elevated to the royal rank of Basilica May 4, 1956 when, contrary to custom, Pope Pius XII personally signed the Papal Brief honoring the church which originated the Sorrowful Mother Novena. The Holy Father also personally blessed the Basilica Canopeum before it was shipped to Chicago. The present magnificent church was started in 1900 and completed two years later. The Apostolic Proclamation of Pope Pius XII granting the rank of Basilica states: "It is well to remember the Novena prayers to the Blessed Mother of God were first compiled and then prayed in this Church and are now used in 2,300 churches throughout the U.S.A. and other parts of the world . . . This Shrine is the most popular church in Chicago, and also in the U.S."

*   *   *

Chicago's other royal church is the Basilica of Queen of All Saints, 6280 Sauganash Avenue. Raised to the rank of Basilica March 26, 1962 by Pope John XIII, this Basilica is considered one of the most beautiful churches in America. In the tradition of Notre Dame of Paris and the shrines at Chartres, Rheims, Rouen, Amiens, the Basilica of Queen of All Saints is built in the ageless style of Gothic. Cathedral-like in appearance, it was planned and designed like one of the old world shrines. Outstanding among its treasures are its windows which rank among the finest examples of stained glass in the 20th Century. The size and power of this great Basilica are suggested by the 100 tons of marble in altar and reredos; the 100 tons of slate on the roof; the 110,000 copper nails to affix the roof slate; the 57,000 pieces in the window of Apparitions, the 33,000 pieces in the mosaic reredos.

IOWA

Dyersville, Iowa is the home of the Basilica of Saint Francis Xavier raised to a Basilica May 11, 1956 by Pope Pius XII, the twelfth U.S. church to receive this honor. Pope Pius honored this church because of its architectural integrity and beauty, and the devotion and zeal of its parishioners. A Masterpiece of special interest is the painting on the ceiling over the main altar.

BASILICAS

KENTUCKY

Covington, Kentucky is the site of Cathedral Basilica of the Assumption, honored with its rank December 8, 1953 by Pope Pius XII. Described as "America's Notre Dame of Paris," this Basilica is rich in art, including paintings by Frank Duveneck, and mosaic Stations of the Cross. Upwards of 70,000 pieces of tile were used in each Station by craftsmen in Venice, Italy.

* * *

Trappist, Kentucky is the home of the Basilica of Our Lady of Gethsemani Abbey. Gethesemani was founded in 1848 by a colony of 40 Cistercian monks on behalf of the Motherhouse Mellery in France. Their church was completed in 1866, and Basilican status was granted May 3, 1949. Available from the Trappist Monks at Gethsemani Abbey, who themselves operate Gethsemani Farms, are fine cheese and fruit cakes made from the best ingredients obtainable. Trappist cheese is truly an epicurean delight.

LOUISIANA

The Basilica of St. Louis, King of France, on Jackson Square, New Orleans, Louisiana, one of the nation's historic landmarks, was elevated to a Basilica December 9, 1964. General Andrew Jackson is the most interesting non-ecclesiastical figure associated with the Cathedral. A footnote in the Cathedral archives reads: "On the eighth day of January, 1915, occurred the famous battle against the British Army, from which the Americans emerged victorious . . ." This "famous battle," at the end of the War of 1812, is a military curiosity because, unknown to the belligerents, the peace treaty had already been signed. When the triumphant Jackson led his men into the rescued city, he went to St. Louis Cathedral and stood at attention during the **Te Deum.**

MARYLAND

The Baltimore, Maryland Co-Cathedral, Minor Basilica of the Assumption of The Blessed Virgin Mary, is the oldest cathedral in the United States and the Mother Church of Catholicism in the nation. It received Basilican rank September 1, 1937. Hanging in the Basilica is the great canvas by Baron Charles de Steuben, painted for Louis XVIII, and presented by the king to the Basilica.

Another heroic canvas in the Basilica is a painting by Baron Pierre Narcisse Gherin, depicting the Blessed Mother holding the broken body of her Divine Son, which Joseph of Arimethea, Nicodemus and their helpers have just taken from the cross. This painting was commissioned by Louis XVIII and given to the Basilica by his successor, Charles X.

BALTIMORE CO-CATHEDRAL, Baltimore, Md., Minor Basilica of the Assumption of the Blessed Virgin Mary, is the oldest Cathedral in the United States, and the Mother Church of Catholicism in the nation.

13

MASSACHUSETTS

The Basilica of Our Lady of Perpetual Help, 1545 Tremont Street, Roxbury, Massachusetts, was raised to its regal rank September 8, 1954 by His Holiness Pius XII. Known to many as the Mission Church, in this hallowed spot are two bases filled with crutches, canes and casts left by cripples who have walked away unaided, by the blind who have found their sight.

MINNESOTA

The Basilica of St. Mary, Minneapolis, Minnesota, has the distinction of the first church in the United States to be raised to the regal rank of Minor Basilica by the Holy See. The honor was conferred by His Holiness, Pope Pius XI on February 1, 1926. This Basilica is a striking example of Modern Renaissance architecture and compares favorably in size, design and liturgical richness with the famous churches of the world.

MISSOURI

St. Louis, Mo., is the home of the Basilica of St. Louis, King of France. This historic church, consecrated in 1834, is part of the Jefferson National Expansion Memorial. In 1841, Pope Gregory XVI granted in perpetuity to this church (known as the Old Cathedral) the same indulgences reserved only for persons visiting the Seven Basilicas in Rome. January 27, 1961, Pope John decreed Basilican status on this famous church.

* * *

The Abbey Church of Conception Abbey, Conception, Missouri, was started in 1882 as the center of the monastery's liturgical life. The Holy Rule of St. Benedict that is the basis of life at Conception began about 1500 years ago in Italy when St. Benedict wrote his Holy Rule. Pope Pius XII raised the church to a Minor Basilica September 14, 1940.

NEW YORK

The Basilica of Our Lady of Victory, Lackawanna, New York, founded by Monsignor Nelson Henry Baker in 1920, was elevated in 1926. The Basilica dome is 251 feet in circumference, exceeded in the United States only by the dome of the Capitol in Washington, D.C.

The Basilica of St. Adalbert is in Buffalo, N.Y., on Stanislaus Street. Its twin tower and cupola are landmarks on the east side of Buffalo. This church traces its history to 1886 and to the zeal of a group of Polish emigrants. In 1907, Pope St. Pius X adjoined the Church of St. Adalbert to St. Peter's Basilica in Rome, granting in perpetuity the privilege of enjoying all the indulgences and spiritual favors which the Vatican Basilica enjoys.

PENNSYLVANIA

Pennsylvania has two Basilicas: Basilica of the Sacred Heart of Jesus, Conewago, elevated June 30, 1962; and the Archabbey Basilica of St. Vincent de Paul, Benedictine Archabbey, Latrobe, elevated August 22, 1955. Pope John XXIII elevated the church at Conewago to Basilica rank because of the Church's history, its beautiful interior and wealth of art works. The Chapel of Relics within the Basilica contains relics of the True Cross and of four Jesuit martyrs, Ignatius, Aloysius, Francis Xavier and Peter Clever.

A main point of interest in Saint Vincent Basilica is the main altar of wide, table-like design so that services can be performed from either side. Two base blocks each weighs 2½ tons, and the cross-slab or mensa weighs 10 tons. The base blocks are of Botticino marble, cream colored with red and black veining. The mensa is Verdi Scuro Fraye marble, dark green with gold veining.

Dr. Leo Ravazzi, a native of Pietrosanto, executed the four sculptured panels on the base blocks. As one looks at the altar from the nave, the right block bears a carving of Moses sacrificing the Pascal Lamb while the left one portrays the impending sacrifice of Isaac by Abraham. Two more panels face the monks' choir. On the right is the sacrifice of Melchisedech and on the left, the sacrifices of Cain and Abel.

WISCONSIN

Milwaukee, Wisconsin's St. Josaphat's Church received its Basilican rank March 10, 1929 from Pope Pius XI. The stones used to build St. Josaphat's in 1900-01 came from the old Chicago Post Office and Court House which had been razed to make way for a new building.

CHAPEL OF THE HOLY CROSS, Sedona, Arizona, is perched on a twin-pinnacled spur of red sandstone 250 feet high. Front wall of the church is a giant cross rising ninety feet from bed rock.

GUIDE TO 200

FAMOUS AMERICAN

CHURCHES, CATHEDRALS,

SHRINES AND BASILICAS

AVE MARIA GROTTO on the campus of St. Barnard College, Cullman, Alabama, displays in concrete miniature, 125 replicas of world famous shrines. Surrounding the Ave Maria Grotto is "Little Jerusalem," the buildings of the Holy Land.

ALABAMA

CULLMAN—Ave Maria Grotto, St. Bernard College, 1 mile off U.S. Highway 31. The creation of a Benedictine monk, Brother Joseph Zoettel, Ave Maria Grotto displays more than 125 miniature replicas of world famous shrines and religious buildings. Among them are: St. Peter's Church, Rome; the California missions, Jerusalem of the Biblical period, Roman miniatures, Noah directing his animals into the Ark, the Tower of Babel, the Hanging Gardens, the Basilica at Lourdes, France. In the center of the four acres of handcrafted miniatures is the huge Grotto. A stonemason constructed it; then Brother Joseph cemented stalactites to the ceiling and ornamented the nine-foot altar with mosaics.

MOBILE—The Basilica of the Immaculate Conception was born of a twenty-by-fifty foot log cabin, built in 1828, and described at that time as a "poor wooden barn, destitute of any kind of ornament." The present magnificent Cathedral-Basilica, marked by its classic portico facing Claiborne street, is an outstandng landmark of downtown Mobile. Majestic twin towers were erected around 1890, and subsequently, imported stained glass windows were added. Early in the morning of March 19, 1954, a fire completely destroyed the sanctuary. During the reconstruction, the damaged stained glass windows were dismantled and shipped to Munich, Germany, where the company that had installed them was able to make restorations from the original cartoons in their files. March 10, 1962, the Cathedral was elevated to the rank of Minor Basilica.

ARIZONA

SEDONA—Chapel of the Holy Cross, Rimrock Road. The Chapel of the Holy Cross, conceived and built by Marguerite Brunswig Staude, the sculptor, to the memory of her parents, is perched on a twin-pinnacled spur of red sandstone about 250 feet high, jutting out of a thousand foot rock wall. The front wall of the church is a giant Cross, rising ninety feet from bed rock, and flanked by huge windows. Inside, the figure of Christ Crucified is suspended from the giant cross. This figure stops one in his tracks. For here, in metal you witness the reality of the words, "He emptied Himself." The mouth is open. Keith Monroe, sculptor of this Christus observed, "Brother still crucifies brother—a continual nourishing of agony and violence. The open mouth is, of course, a protest and a call to end this inhumanity. The viewer **should** be horrified by this aspect and be moved to ends of peace and humanity by it. Reaction, even against this piece, is good . . . Man too often is more anxious to escape facing his guilt and inhumanity—to favor a more relaxed superficial attitude. The Church **is** a power for peace and love, but it must be a militant power, outraged by outrage, strong and clear in protest to inhumanity, aware of and sympathetic to the agonies mankind suffers every day." The vision for this church came to Marguerite Brunswig Staude in 1932 as she looked at the newly completed Empire State Building in New York City. When viewed from a certain angle, a cross seemed to impose itself through the core of the structure. From this came the first sketch for a cruciform church. Miss Staude and Frank Lloyd Wright interpreted the sketch. Wright built the first architectural model with the articulated cross and, in 1937, plans were made and accepted to build the church in Budapest overlooking the Danube. World War II ended the project. In 1952, the spectacular site at Sedona, Arizona was selected and, in April 1956, this national shrine "where God can be worshipped as a contemporary" was completed.

TUCSON—Saint Augustine's Cathedral, Stone Avenue, downtown Tucson, dates from the Spanish beginnings of Tucson; it grew from the tiny adobe chapel of the padres that was in the presidio in the 1700's to the nationally known mission-style Cathedral of today. The interior murals and windows show a variety of sources, from the native talent of the Mexican artist to that of Munich. Maria Koch suggests that "the visitor with leisure will discover the sensitivity of the work in such things as the flying angel with upward pointed wings urging him to love the Lord, and the standing angel with downward pointing wings urging him to love his neighbor." Especially noteworthy are the painting of St. Bartholomew attributed to Guiseppe Ribera, Madrid; and the life-size crucifix of the twelfth or thirteenth century from Pamplona.

TUCSON—The Mission San Xavier del Bac (Saint Xavier of the Springs), 9 miles south of Tucson, was founded in 1700, and is one of the fine mission churches of the Southwest. It was administered by the Jesuits for 67 years. In 1783 the Franciscan friars began to build a church that the Indians called "White Dove of the Desert." The baroque front of the church, between two graceful towers, features complicated designs in brick and plaster work.

Three balconies at the front of the church once allowed distinguished guests and their ladies to gaze down on the Indian dances performed on the feast days of the mission.

TUMACACORI—Tumacacori National Monument, 48 miles south of Tucson and 18 miles north of Nogales on U.S. 89, is a typical old mission church which illustrates Spanish colonial endeavor and commemorates the introduction of Christianity into what is now southern Arizona. The Mission of San Jose de Tumacacori was a northern outpost of a mission chain constructed by Franciscan priests in the late 1700's on sites established by the Jesuits in what was then the Mexican Province of Sonora. As a reminder that Spain was active on the frontier in the Southwest long before the United States became a nation, Tumacacori remains today a symbol of the faith, courage and vigor of the early missionary priests and of the loyalty and devotion of the Indian converts.

YARNELL—The Yarnell Shrine of St. Joseph of the Mountains, Route 89, 30 miles southwest of Prescott, was erected by the Catholic Action League of Arizona in 1939. The many life-size statues of the shrine are made of reinforced concrete; in the hands of the late Felix Lucero, this rigid medium was handled with subtlety, grace and realism. Christ sitting alone at the table of the Last Supper is particularly impressive. The Shrine also features life-size figures of the Way of the Cross erected in honor of the soldiers of World War I.

ARKANSAS

EUREKA SPRINGS—Christ of the Ozarks, a mammoth statue seven stories high, with an armspread of 65 feet, overlooks Eureka Springs from Magnetic Mountain, and can be viewed from as far as the human eye can reach.

EUREKA SPRINGS—St. Elizabeth's Catholic Church, off City Route 62, on Crescent Drive, entered through the bell tower, is one of the top ten attractions in America listed by the American Travel Service; featured in Ripley's "Believe-It-Or-Not."

LITTLE ROCK—St. Andrews Cathedral, 617 Louisiana Street. Two towers, each 220 feet high, dominate the English Gothic architecture of this Cathedral. The church was built of native granite, quarried at Fourche Mountain, in 1878. The Cathedral measures 140 feet in length and 86 feet across the transept. The interior is finished in native wood.

CALIFORNIA

FRESNO—St. John the Baptist Cathedral, 2800 Mariposa Street, known as the "Cathedral in the Valley," was built in 1882, rebuilt in 1902 and, when the diocese of Monterey-Fresno was created in 1922, St. John's was made its cathedral. The first session of the court in the canonization process for Padre Junipero Serra was held in this cathedral. The exquisite murals on the walls are the work of the Italian artist, L. Brusatori, who had come to the United States to work on the San Francisco exposition.

LOS ANGELES—Saint Vibiana Cathedral, Main and Second Streets. The general plan of this cathedral was suggested by the Church of the Puerto de San Miguel in Barcelona. The church is named for a third century virgin and martyr whose body is enshrined above the main altar. The body was brought from the Roman catacombs in 1854.

SACRAMENTO—Cathedral of the Blessed Sacrament, 1017 11th Street, was completed in 1889 in the Italian Renaissance style. Its structure is cruciform, 208 feet long and 114 feet high. The stained glass windows of the church are typical of Viennese artistry. Especially noteworthy is a full-size replica of Raphael's "Sistine Madonna," donated by Mrs. Leland Stanford.

JOLON—The Mission San Antonio de Padua, Hunter Liggett Military Reservation. Leave Highway 101 at King City or Bradley. This mission was founded in 1771 and restored in 1949 with funds made available through the Hearst Foundation. The mission possessed a remarkable irrigation system and the remains of the ditches can still be seen. A feature of the mission church is its facade and vaulted ceiling made entirely of burnt brick. The plaster floor of the church is unique for a California mission.

LOMPOC—Mission La Purisima, founded in 1787, was rebuilt by the Civilian Conservation Corps in the 1930's. This most extensive and accurate restoration of a California mission has been designated a State Historical Monument. The mission stands on a 966-acre monument which includes the old mission water system. The visitor should take note of the church's colonnade of 18 fluted columns.

THE NAVE OF LAPURISIMA MISSION, Lompoc, Calif., founded 1787.
Colonnade of fluted columns is shown in exterior photo below.

SAN LUIS REY DE FRANCIA, "the Old Mission," at San Luis Rey, Calif., contains rare art treasures. Designated a U.S. Historical Monument.

OCEANSIDE—San Luis Rey de Francia, Mission Road, 3½ miles east of Oceanside, once the largest Indian mission in the New World (its farm and pasture lands extended for a radius of 15 miles) has been designated a United States Historical Monument as well as a California State Historical Monument. The mission was founded in 1789 and, after its secularization by the Mexican government in 1834, was returned to the Church by an official deed signed by Abraham Lincoln. This deed may be seen in the mission museum. The museum contains rare art treasures and has the largest collection of Spanish vestments in the United States.

SANTA BARBARA—Mission Santa Barbara. The old church of this mission is among the most photographed buildings in the country. Founded in 1786, Santa Barbara has long been known as the "Queen of the Missions." It is situated high on a hill with the backdrop of the Santa Ines Mountains, and a sloping plain runs down to the sea from its feet. The mission church and the museum contain priceless art works, original mission documents, and various artifacts.

SAN DIEGO—Cathedral of Saint Joseph, 1535 Third Avenue. Fourteen cents bought the site of the Cathedral in 1867. It stands in Old Town, the settlement west of the old Mission San Diego de Alcala. The church was built in 1874 and is Spanish in architecture. Its first pastor described the parish boundaries as "the Pacific Ocean and the Colorado River."

SAN FRANCISCO—At the corner of California and Grant, in Chinatown, Old St. Mary's was the first building erected as a Cathedral in California. Old St. Mary's served the Archdiocese of San Francisco in that capacity from 1854 to 1891. Once the city's most prominent building, much of its stone work was quarried and cut in China and its brick brought around the Horn in sailing ships. Old St. Mary's is California Registered Historical Landmark No. 810.

Missions
Franciscan friars brought Christianity to California in 1769. By 1823, the friars had built a chain of 21 missions, a day's travel on horseback apart, from San Diego in the south to Sonoma in the north. These missions flourished until 1834 when the Mexican government secularized them. The churches, schools and farms fell into ruin and decay until they were returned to the Church

25

following California's statehood in 1848. The missions have now been partially or wholly restored and can be visited in or near the following cities.

CARMEL—Mission San Carlos Borromeo, one mile south of Carmel near the intersection of State Highway 1 and the Rio Road. This mission is of special interest because it is the burial place of Padre Junipero Serra, foremost of the Franciscan missionaries in California. It is the second oldest mission in the state, founded in 1770, and in 1960 was raised to the status of a Minor Basilica by Pope John XIII. Noteworthy is the Shrine of Our Lady of Belen, the Conquistadora of California. The statue was brought from Mexico by Padre Serra.

FREMONT—Mission of San Jose Guadalupe, 18 miles south of San Francisco, stands near the southern end of the San Francisco Bay. The church houses many souvenirs of the old Franciscan mission church. The old olive orchard, gardens and Indian graveyard make this mission well worth a visit.

SANTA CLARA—Mission Santa Clara de Assis is one of the few missions to pass permanently from Franciscan control. It was ceded to the Jesuits in 1854 and they now conduct the University of Santa Clara on the old mission grounds. They also maintain the de Saisset Art Museum and Gallery open to tourists. One transcept of the mission church is known as the Shrine of the Miraculous Crucifix. The life-size work of Christ in agony on the Cross is the most hallowed object of worship in mission history. The painting of the Holy Family was done by Guiseppe Riva of Bergamo, Italy, and three statues in the church are the work of Guido Mayer, the man who, for many years, enacted the role of Judas in the Passion Play of Oberammergau, Germany.

SANTA CRUZ—Mission of Santa Cruz. A new church marks the original site of this mission, founded in 1791. Three statues, a few dark paintings and several dark vestments survive from the old church.

SAN DIEGO—Mission San Diego de Alcala, 11005 Friars Road. This was California's first mission, established here on July 16, 1769. It was founded by the famous Padre Junipero Serra and the mission museum contains memorials of the great "Conquistador of the Cross." The mission also has the oldest graveyard in California where the state's first martyr is buried.

SAN FERNANDO—Mission San Fernando, 15151 Mission Boulevard. Noted for the 21 arches which enclose its expansive porch, the convent is the largest original structure that remains in the California mission chain. The mission chapel, also an original building, was completed in 1806. Authentic Indian designs enhance the inside walls which appear to be leaning outward because they are six feet thick at the bottom and taper to 3½ feet near the top.

SAN LUIS OBISPO—Mission San Luis Obispo de Tolosa, named for St. Louis, the bishop of Toulouse, France, stands at the half-way point in the mission chain "In the heart of the Mission Trails." The mission church is a splendid example of unadorned Baroque and its museum and gardens make it well worth a visit.

SAN MIGUEL—Mission San Miguel Archangel, just off Highway 101, 7 miles north of Pasa Rables. Boasting the best preserved interior of all the California missions, Mission San Miguel Archangel was founded in 1797. The roof tiles of the church are the original ones, and the woodwork in the interior is a fine example of mission carpenter and cabinet work. The interior of the church was decorated by Esteban Munros, famous Spanish artist. In the sanctuary is the "Wishing Chair" favored by Indian maidens in their search for a husband.

SAN RAFAEL—The Mission San Rafael Archangel, founded in 1817, was the second to the last founded in the mission chain and never had an opportunity to flourish before secularization in 1834.

SOLEDAD—Mission Nuestra Senora de la Soledad, founded in 1791, is the only one in the chain of California missions that has not been restored. Fiestas are held annually in October to finance the eventual restoration.

SOLVANG—The Mission of Santa Ines is often called the "Hidden Gem of the Missions." Founded in 1804, it contains treasures of seventeenth, eighteenth, and nineteenth century Mexican art as well as bright Indian decorations.

SONOMA—Mission San Francisco Solano is northernmost in the mission chain and the last to be founded. It was established in 1823 and became the only one established under Mexican rule. It has been designated as part of a California State Historical Monument along with an old Spanish garrison and barracks.

CALIFORNIA

SAN FRANCISCO—Mission San Francisco de Assis (Mission Dolores), 3321 16th Street, was founded in 1776, five days before the Declaration of Independence was signed. It is the oldest structure in the city of San Francisco. It is one of the few buildings that survived the earthquake and fire of 1906. The roof timbers are redwood lashed together by rawhide. The redwood ceiling beams were carved by Indians and decorated with vegetable colors. A huge redwood cross stands in the cemetery. The mission altar and bells came from Mexico and the tabernacle from Manila. Adjoining the original mission is Mission Dolores Basilica. The main altar is of Numidian marble; around the nave are mosaic medallions with pictures of the twelve apostles.

SAN GABRIEL—The Mission San Gabriel Archangel, San Gabriel, nine miles east of Los Angeles, was founded in 1771 by the Franciscans. In 1908, control of the mission was turned over to the Claretian Fathers, a missionary order. In this mission are a series of paintings by an unknown aboriginal artist who faithfully reproduced the Stations of the Cross on sailcloth. The mission has the oldest painting of Our Lady of Sorrows in North America.

SAN JUAN—Mission of San Juan Bautista, founded by Franciscans in 1797, is now in the hands of the Maryknoll Missionaries. The church is unique because it is not built in the long quadrangle which was traditional of the Spanish missions, but is more cathedral-like in structure.

SAN JUAN CAPISTRANO—Mission San Juan Capistrano, 60 miles southeast of Los Angeles, immortalized in song and story, was founded in 1776 and is the seventh oldest in the mission chain. For years the swallows of Capistrano have regularly left the mission for the south on October 23, and have just as regularly returned to the mission on March 19, St. Joseph's Day. During the spring and summer they live in mudnests built in the old mission's walls.

VENTURA—The Mission San Buenaventura was founded in 1782. A visit at Christmas time is especially memorable for then the mission gardens blaze with poinsettias.

ALTAR OF THE CATHOLIC NAVE, inter-faith chapel of the U.S. Air Force Academy, Colorado.

DENVER—U. S. Air Force Academy Chapel. The 17 aluminum-covered spires of Academy Chapel dominate the 17,900-acre site of the United States Air Force Academy. Protestant, Catholic and Jewish services can be held simultaneously in the Chapel in separate worship areas. The Catholic Chapel, located on the terrace level, accommodates 500 persons. The wall behind the Altar is an abstract mural of varying shades of blue, turquoise, rose and gray glass tessera. Superimposed on the mural are two marble figures: "Our Lady of the Skies" (The Blessed Mother) and the Guardian Angel. Above and between the two figures is a marble dove, symbolic of the Holy Ghost. A single slab of polished marble forms the Altar. The fourteen Stations of the Cross were carved from four-inch slabs of marble. Their backgrounds are covered with the same multi-colored tessera of the reredos mural.

COLORADO

DENVER—Mother Frances Xavier Cabrini Shrine. From Denver, drive west to Colfax (route 40) and continue until road reaches mouth of Mt. Vernon Canyon. Here, at a "Y", road divides. Keep to right on Route 40 leading up canyon. One and one-third miles from the "Y" is a sign reading Mother Cabrini Shrine. This Shrine was erected in memory of the first canonized saint (1946) who was an American citizen. In 1912, Mother Cabrini sought a summer home for the use of the Queen of Heaven Orphanage, Denver, which she founded in 1904. Her search led into the foothills west of Denver where, with her own hands, Mother Cabrini selected white rocks and fashioned the image of a heart upon the ground in honor of the Sacred Heart of Jesus. The rocks remain today as she placed them. Later, as the sisters collected stones for the children's home, they discovered that apparently there was no water on the property. When this was reported to Mother Cabrini, she said: "Nonsense" and tapped a stone with a staff she carried. Under the rock was found an unfailing source of spring water. A Stairway of Prayer leads to a statue of the Sacred Heart. Stations of the Cross and mysteries of the Rosary adorn sides of the stairway.

DENVER—Cathedral of the Immaculate Conception, Northwest corner of Logan and Colfax. Two towering spires mark the Gothic architecture of Denver's downtown Cathedral. Designed by Leon Coquard of Detroit, this Cathedral is a foremost example of French Gothic in the United States. Interior pillars, walls and confessionals are faced partly with white veined Colorado marble; the altars, pulpit, Bishop's throne and statues are of Carrara marble. The main altar, rising 30 feet above the sanctuary floor, has for its main central figure, far above the tabernacle, a marble reproduction of Murillo's "Immaculate Conception." Under the table of the altar, paneled between marble pillars, is a marble reproduction of Da Vinci's "Last Supper." The Cathedral is famous for its stained glass executed in Munich, Germany. Deep toned in color, minute in detail, they tell of the principal events in the life of the Savior and Our Lady. Twenty thousand pieces of stained glass were used to form the windows that occupy most of the east and west transept walls of the building.

CONNECTICUT

HARTFORD—Cathedral of St. Joseph is the successor to the old Cathedral, destroyed by fire in 1956. Spectacularly effective are the series of huge (67'x13.5') windows placed down the nave. Slab glass, an inch thick in a wide range of colors, was used by Jean Barillet of Paris to create the windows. Tommaso Peccini sculptured the frieze in travertine over the three principal main entrance doors, in the center of which is an heroic likeness of St. Joseph. Gleb Derujinsky sculptured the four archangels integrated into the tripod-form Baldachin. Behind the altar rises a tremendous reredos of ceramic, 80 feet high and 40 feet wide, believed to be the largest work of its kind in the world. Designed by Enzo Assneza, it has as its subject "The Saviour in Glory."

NORWICH—St. Patrick's Cathedral, 213 Broadway, is the church nurtured in its first years around the 1880's by the "ten-cents-a-week" club. Ten cents a week was asked as a contribution from each working family, and this was how St. Patrick's was financed. The Cathedral's Bells of St. Patrick were the gift of John Byrne, a member of the famous theatrical family, in 1900; fifty years later, an electric bell ringer was installed, the gift of a member of the Jewish faith, and a friend of St. Patrick's.

THE FAMOUS FRANCISCAN Memorial Church of the Holy Land, Washington, D.C., contains replicas of the holy shrines in Jordan, Israel, Egypt and Syria.

NATIONAL SHRINE OF The Immaculate Conception, Washington, D.C., largest Catholic Church in the U.S. Built in the form of a Latin cross, the Shrine on its outside walls has 137 pieces of sculpture and ten mosaics, a permanent museum of works by American artists.

WASHINGTON, D.C.

NATIONAL SHRINE OF THE IMMACULATE CONCEPTION—
4th and Michigan Aves., N.E. This is the largest Catholic Church
in the United States and the seventh largest in the world. Built
as were medieval cathedrals, without steel skeleton or framework,
the Shrine is designed in the form of the Latin cross. Its architecture is in the spirit of Byzantine and Romanesque. On the outside
walls are 137 separate pieces of sculpture, a permanent museum
of some of the works of great American artists. On a balcony
within the huge Roman entrance arch stands a statue of Mary
Immaculate with Angels by Ivan Mestrovic. Among the mosaics
are The Assumption, copy of Titian's Assumption, sent to the
Shrine by Pope John XXIII, and a mosaic copy of Murillo's Immaculate Conception given by Pope Benedict XV and Pope Pius
XI. Gleaming red and gold beyond the marble altar, on the north
apse wall, is a mosaic showing in mighty proportions Christ the
Lord of the Universe. Artist John de Rosen created this mosaic,
which occupies 3,610 square feet. Luci Baines Johnson, 19, younger
daughter of President Johnson, was married in the National Shrine
on August 6, 1966, to Patrick John Nugent. This was the first
Catholic wedding in which a President's daughter was the bride.

**FRANCISCAN MONASTERY, MEMORIAL CHURCH OF THE
HOLY LAND—**Mount St. Sepulchre, 1400 Quincy Street, N.E.
The Franciscan Monastery, also known as the Commissariat of the
Holy Land for the United States, contains reproductions of Sacred
Shrines of the Holy Land. These include: Our Divine Saviour's
Tomb as it is at the present day in Jerusalem; the Stone of
Annointing which covers the place where the body of Our Lord
was anointed and prepared for burial; Altar of Calvary, replica
of the one which stands over the place where the Cross was set in
the sacred rock of Calvary; Grotto of Nazareth, reproduction of
the Shrine of the Annunciation as it is today in the village of
Nazareth in Galilee; the Grotto of Bethlehem, Grotto of Gethsemane, Tomb of the Blessed Virgin, and Chapel of the Ascension.
To these replicas, the Holy See has accorded the same Indulgences
that may be obtained at the Holy Places in Palestine. The Franciscan Monastery is cared for by members of the Order of Friars
Minor, founded by St. Francis in 1209. Since then the Sacred Places
have been entrusted to the guardianship of the Franciscan Order.

ST. MATTHEW'S CATHEDRAL—1725 Rhode Island Avenue, N.W. In the chapel of St. Francis Assisi are LaFarge frescoes of St. Francis and St. Clare, plus two more of St. Francis receiving the stigmata. Mosaics in the four pendentives under the dome were executed in Rome under the direction of Salvatore Lascari. Each is over 400 feet in width. The statues in the Chapel of St. Joseph are of sculptured wood overlaid with gold leaf. The statue in the Lady Chapel is of Caen Marble carved in Paris. The frontal of the High Altar is of white marble decorated with floral designs in colored insets. This decoration, which is characteristic of the Indian decoration in the Taj Mahal at Agra, was executed in India, and is probably unique in the United States. On the morning of November 25, 1963, the flag-draped casket containing the body of the slain President, John F. Kennedy, was placed on a caisson in the Capitol Building, then moved in procession to the White House, and then to St. Matthew's Cathedral. Richard Cardinal Cushing of Boston, an old friend of the Kennedy family, celebrated a pontifical low mass in the Cathedral. The cortege proceeded to Arlington Cemetery where the first Catholic President of the United States was buried.

FLORIDA

ST. AUGUSTINE—Mission of Nombre De Dios. The old Spanish Mission preserves the landing site of America's first Founding Fathers, and the spot on which stood the first Christian Mission and Parish in the United States. On September 8, 1565, Spanish Admiral Pedro Menendez landed to found an American settlement. Father Francisco Lopez, one of four diocesan priests accompanying the expedition, offered a Mass of Thanksgiving. It was the first Parish Mass, and the first community act of Christian religion in the United States. Today, on the old Mission grounds, a rustic altar commemorates that first Mass. The pioneer Father Lopez is memorialized in an heroic statue executed by the late Yugoslav sculptor, Ivan Mestrovic. A small chapel stands where the first Mission chapel was built four centuries ago. In the Quadricentennial year of 1965, in the waters adjoining the Mission where the Spanish ships lay at anchor 400 years before, a 200-foot-high stainless steel illuminated cross was erected to remind men on land and sea of the religious beginnings of the United States.

THE "GREAT CROSS — Beacon of the Faith," located at the Mission of Nombre de Dios in St. Augustine, Florida, this nation's oldest city, marks the site where the cross of Christianity was first planted in this nation over 400 years ago. Erected "to remind all men who pass through or enter St. Augustine of our country's religious beginnings," says Mission Director Father Michael Gannon, the 208-foot cross is visible from some 23 miles by sea for large vessels and 19 miles for smaller craft, and from highways leading into St. Augustine.

CATHEDRAL OF ST. AUGUSTINE, St. Augustine, Florida, is the parish church of Cathedral Parish, founded 1565, oldest Catholic parish in the United States.

ST. AUGUSTINE—The Cathedral of St. Augustine, built 1791-1797 under Spanish rule, is the oldest existing church building in Cathedral Parish, which is the oldest Catholic parish in the United States. The nation's oldest Catholic parish was founded in 1565 by Father Francisco Lopez de Mendoza Grajales, chaplain of the fleet of Spanish Admiral Pedro Menendez de Aviles. Menendez and a band of Spanish settlers landed here September 8, 1565, and attended a Mass in honor of the Blessed Virgin, celebrated by Father Lopez. The Admiral named his settlement St. Augustine. To Father Lopez goes credit as the first parish priest in the United States. This was forty-two years before the English settled in Virginia, fifty-five years before the Pilgrims landed at Plymouth, two hundred years before California's great Catholic missions, and two centuries before our American Declaration of Independence was signed. Typical of many churches built by the Spanish during the 18th Century, the walls of the facade swoop up in graceful ogee curves. The church was built of coquina rock. Inside, the atmosphere is of old Spain, sombre, chaste and austere. Unusual feature is the dark wood flat ceiling paneled in a geometric design, and supported by trusses rather than visible columns of any kind. Framed in an alcove formed by white marble Corinthian columns supporting a depressed arch is the high altar of Carrara marble. This Italian Renaissance altar was designed by James Renwick and carved by J. Massey Rhind.

SARASOTA—Sarasota Museum of the Cross, U.S. Highway 301 (Tamiami Trail) at the interesection of U.S. 41. This museum is the work of Ben Stahl, artist and illustrator. He has painted 15 almost-life-size oils for "The Way of the Cross." The paintings cover the last five hours of Jesus' life, from condemnation before Pontius Pilate to the placing of His Body in the tomb. The resurrection is also illustrated. The exhibit includes a collection of more than 200 crosses and crucifixes, most of them in silver, handcrafted in Spain.

GEORGIA

SAVANNAH—Cathedral of St. John the Baptist, LaFayette Square, is an art-rich tribute to the oldest religion in Georgia, Roman Catholicism, introduced here by European explorers in the early 1500's. Two golden crosses atop the lofty spires dominate the Savannah skyline. Forty-three stained glass windows, most of which were executed by Innsbruck Glassmakers in Austrian Tyrol and installed around 1900, and mural-paintings combine in unique beauty. Two of the most spectacular windows depict the Ascension of Our Lord Jesus Christ (North Transept) and Assumption of the Blessed Virgin Mary (South Transept). The Cathedral's great rose window is a quatrefoil in which St. Cecilia is represented with her emblem, the portable organ. Ten radiations, each terminating in a medallion, and ten outer foliated rosettes are other main elements in this masterpiece. The Cathedral's murals rank among the best in the United States. The four largest, in the main sanctuary are devoted to the four writers of the Gospels, Saints Matthew, Mark, Luke and John.

IDAHO

CATALDO—The Old Coeur d'Alene Mission is a shrine to three Jesuits who labored among the Coeur d'Alene Indians. The town itself is named for one of the three priests and the chapel stands as a memorial to their work. The three priests, companions of Father De Smet, constructed the chapel of timbers and one of the Jesuits painted several pictures and carved three of the statues that are found within.

ILLINOIS

BELLEVILLE—The National Shrine of Our Lady of the Snows. Entrance and exit to the Shrine Grounds is along U.S. route 460 between Belleville and East St. Louis, Illinois. This highway is easily found on the Illinois end of the three Mississippi River bridges from downtown St. Louis, Mo., and the Shrine is 15 minutes from there. Route 460 bypasses Belleville to the south of the city. This shrine is directed by the Oblate Fathers and is the world's largest outdoor Shrine honoring Mary. This is a pilgrimage center—a public center of adoration of the Blessed Sacrament as well as an open house for informal retreats and daily year-round

NATIONAL SHRINE OF Our Lady of the Snows, Belleville, Ill., the world's largest outdoor shrine honoring Our Lady. At the Shrine are a tripodal M-shaped outdoor Altar, and an amphitheatre for 20,000 people on a 2,200-acre site.

center for Holy Mass, Communion, Confession and various special blessings. Devotion to Our Lady of the Snows began more than sixteen centuries ago in Rome when the people of the Eternal City awoke on the morning of August 5, 352 A.D. to find the Esquiline Hill covered with snow. The snow had been predicted by the Blessed Mother when she appeared to Pope Liberius and to a noble couple who prayed for a special intention. The couple arranged for a church, the original Shrine of Our Lady of the Snows, to be built on the spot where the snow had fallen. Thousands of pilgrims from the far corners of the earth have journeyed to the Shrine to intercede with Mary for special intentions. The Shrine is a tripodal M-shaped outdoor Altar and amphitheatre accommodating 20,000 people on a 2200-acre tract on the bluffs overlooking the Mississippi Valley. Under the dome, behind the altar, is a richly ornamented Perpetual Adoration Chapel. Behind the central structure are Shrines of the Fifteen Mysteries of the Rosary. Four electrically operated bells, erected over a reflection pool in a meditation garden on the crest of a hill overlooking the outdoor Shrine altar, ring the Angelus. High point of the year is the Solemn Novena of Our Lady of the Snows from July 28 to August 5.

BELLEVILLE—St. Peter's Cathedral, 330 South Third Street, is recognized for the beauty and symbolism of its liturgical art. The

Stations of the Cross are carved out of smoked marble. The Sanctuary ceiling is gold leaf with the poppy leaf symbolizing Propagation of the Faith. Surrounding each section of poppy leaves in each Sanctuary arch is an endless border of crosses representing the endless number of martyrs. In the top center of each side wall is a figure of an adoring angel on olive background; olives symbolize the earth and this background is olive because it joins the two lower sections of mosaic frescoes of earthly events of St. Peter's life. Mosaic fresco backgrounds on silver and gold leaf form a shrine-like setting for statues of the Sacred Heart and of St. Anthony. A suspended Crucifix in the Baptistry portrays the Agony of Christ in twisted contortions.

CHICAGO—National Shrine of St. Jude, 3200 East 91st Street, established by the Claretian Fathers in 1929, is the first major Shrine in the United States dedicated to St. Jude. This Mother Shrine is in Our Lady of Guadalupe Church in the "South Chicago" section of Chicago. Many people have learned about St. Jude through Danny Thomas, popular comedian-entertainer, who directed a campaign to build St. Jude's Hospital in Memphis, Tennessee.

CHICAGO—Cathedral of the Holy Name, 730 N. Wabash, mother-church of the Catholic Archdiocese of Chicago, was built in 1874. It has been the scene of many solemn functions, including the Eucharistic Congress in 1926. The statue of Our Lady of the Holy Name, carved by an unknown sculptor, graces the side-altar. This statue of white "statuario" Carrara marble, is translucent.

CHICAGO—Basilica of Queen of All Saints, 6280 Sauganash Avenue, is built in the ageless style of Gothic. Outstanding among the treasures for which the Basilica is noted are its windows, which rank among the finest examples of stained glass in the twentieth century. Twelve double lancet windows illumine and adorn the nave, two groups of six on each side. The title of the subject or saint is incorporated in each medallion.

CHICAGO—The Basilica of Our Lady of Sorrows, 3121 W. Jackson Boulevard, achieved this rare and royal rank May 4, 1956, when Pope Pius XII signed the Papal Brief elevating Our Lady of Sorrows Church to Basilica Minor. In signing the Basilica proclamation personally, the Holy Father made this statement: "I want to honor the city of Chicago and the Servants of Mary who have done so much to spread devotion to the Sorrowful Virgin." The

BASILICA OF OUR LADY of Sorrows, Chicago, the home of the Sorrowful Mother Novena. The Novena prayer book, originated here, has gone into 7 million copies in 31 languages.

Basilica, erected by the Servite Fathers in 1890, is also known as the National Shrine of Our Sorrowful Mother, where the Sorrowful Mother Novena originated in 1937, and whence the Novena has spread throughout the world. From a parish devotion, the Novena grew until it has been described as the "religious phenomenon of the age." Material evidence of the impact of the Novena is gained from the fact that the Novena prayerbook, "Queen of Martyrs," has gone into 16 editions, involving more than 7 million copies in 31 languages. Novena services are held every Friday evening, but come early. 75,000 people have been known to stand in line waiting to get inside the Basilica for the devotion. The Basilica itself is a magnificent and imposing church. In the sanctuary are two of the symbols of the Basilica's royal rank: The Canopeum, a 14-foot umbrella, made of twelve long strips of cloth alternating in yellow and scarlet colors; and the Basilica Bell.

CHICAGO—St. Jude Thaddeus Shrine, 1909 South Ashland Avenue. For many centuries all the bodily remains of St. Jude Thaddeus, except the arm bones, have rested in St. Peter's Basilica. The forearm is the possession of St. Jude Thaddeus Shrine. Public devotions to St. Jude have been held daily at this Shrine for over 35 years. The relic is contained in a silver casting of a life-size forearm mounted on a metal base and complete with a partially open hand. The relic is viewed through a sealed glass section in the silver form. St. Jude Thaddeus Shrine is regarded as foremost among shrines to honor this Saint. The altar, the massive life-sized group of 10 figures in marble, the rich mosaic ceiling, combine to make this Shrine a majestic testimonial.

CHICAGO—National Shrine of the Little Flower, Woodlawn Avenue and 64th St. The interior of the National Shrine of the Little Flower is built around the symbol of St. Therese, the rose, and even the lighting fixtures are in the form of rosebushes. Among the relics and souvenirs of the Saint preserved at the Shrine are a crucifix made from the tall rose tree that grew in the monastery garden at Lisieux, France, a chair used by Therese in her cell, a tambourine she played with as a child and a map of America that she drew at the age of 12. In the chapel a casket of crystal and gold holds a branch of five roses. Each rose contains a major relic of St. Therese. This is the largest collection of her relics outside of France.

MELROSE PARK—Calvary Hill Shrine, 14 miles from Chicago, 7 miles from LaGrange. Two blocks east of Mannheim Road between Lake and North Avenue. Entrance on 37th Avenue. This Shrine is conducted by the Scalabrini Fathers, and has, in the past twenty-five years, become the center of attraction and devotion for hundreds of thousands of tourists and pilgrims. Calvary Hill is the dominant attraction at the Shrine. High atop this hill is the bronze group depicting the Crucifixion scene. The life-size figures of the Mother of God, St. John and St. Mary Magdalene beneath the cross portray Christ's enormous suffering. Leading up the front side of Calvary Hill to the Crucifixion scene are the Holy Stairs, replica of the Scala Santa kept in Rome. At the base of Calvary Hill is the Via Matris, the seven Sorrowful Stations of Our Lady and, around the lagoon facing the Holy Stairs, are bronze outdoor Stations of the Cross. The Shrine is available for day pilgrimages, day retreats and Communion breakfasts. Arrangements for group pilgrimages: Calvary Hill Shrine Director, Sacred Heart Seminary, 39th and Division St., Melrose Park. Phone FI 4-8999. The Calvary Hill Passion Play, hour long outdoor sacred pageant tracing Our Lord's passion and death, is presented seven times during the summer. Seating for 2,000. Write or call: Passion Play Ticket Office, Sacred Heart Seminary, Melrose Park.

MUNDELEIN—The Benedictine Sanctuary of Perpetual Adoration of Our Lady of the Blessed Sacrament, Route 176 (Park Avenue at Sayre), is the memorial to the 28th International Eucharistic Congress, (Chicago, June 1926), the first held in the United States. Perpetual Exposition of the Blessed Sacrament began June 7, 1928 and from that day the Benedictine Sisters of Perpetual Adoration have been offering uninterrupted prayers by day and keeping unbroken vigil by night. The Sanctuary is rich in marble, mosaics executed in Innsbruck, Austria; enamel art, statuary, stained glass. The monstrance, five feet two inches in height, was fashioned from gifts of jewelry.

SPRINGFIELD—Cathedral of the Immaculate Conception, 524 Lawrence Avenue, East, was developed in the stately Greek Revival style, and executed in Mankato stone. The church proper is Basilican, the clerestory carried on rows of Siena columns in the Greek Ionic style. Above the Rose Tavernelle wainscot are set the mosaic Stations of the Cross of minute pieces imported from Venice. The windows of the Cathedral are mosaics of finely cut translucent glass, a radical departure from European stain glass. The windows are built, not of lead but of copper. A unique feature of these windows: at night they appear as mosaic panels showing the picture in full color and detail. Among the windows on the Gospel side is one of Father Marquette, who on December 8, 1674 celebrated the first Mass in Chicago approximately where the Wrigley Building now stands. Father Marquette discovered the Mississippi River and named it the River of the Immaculate Conception.

INDIANA

INDIANAPOLIS—St. Rita's Church, 19th and Martindale, typifies the elegance of simplicity. The communion rail, the prie dieus and sanctuary windows are bronze. The wood-carved flying statuary and Stations were made in Italy. Pillars and pylons flanking the altar are Verde Antique Marble; the Altars and Baptismal Font are Verde Lenco; the pulpit, predella and sedilia are Fastastico Arni. This pattern of green is carried into the terrazzo floors. The theme of the Church—religious sacrifice—is depicted in the stained glass windows.

IOWA

DES MOINES—St. Ambrose Cathedral offers fine stained glass windows. Because of their design and authentic historical detail, these windows are often the object of study by students of Church history. The six historical windows present virtually an entire course in the history of the development of the Catholic Church in America including, of course, considerable representation of the Church in Iowa. The ten Sanctuary windows portray the life of Christ in episodic detail.

DUBUQUE—St. Raphael's Cathedral, 231 Bluff Street. Among the many points of interest in St. Raphael's Cathedral is a child's casket containing the bones of a young, early Christian martyr. This boy, Saint Cessianus, was martyred during the reign of the Roman Emperor Diocletian. He reportedly was killed by wild beasts with his parents and other members of his family in the Roman Amphitheatre. The child's age at the time of his death was believed to be between 7 and 9 years. This relic was given to Bishop Matthias Loras by Pope Pius VIII who reigned from 1830 to 1846. At that time, Bishop Loras was touring Europe for the purpose of recruiting young priests and theologians for his Diocese in the new world. The body of Saint Cessianus is located in a visible casket beneath the altar of the Sacred Heart in the northeast corner of the Cathedral.

DYERSVILLE—The Basilica of Saint Francis Xavier became, in 1956, the twelfth U.S. church to receive the royal rank of Basilica. Pope Pius XII conferred this honor because of the architectural integrity and beauty of the church, and the devotion and zeal of its parishioners. A masterpiece of special interest is the painting on the ceiling over the main altar. The central figure, representing the radiant Lamb of God, is surrounded by celestial angels. To the right are saints of the Old Testament and to the left are saints of the New Testament. The wooden crosses on the twin spires were covered with 23 carat gold leaf in 1953.

EACH YEAR, more than 100,000 people visit the Grotto of Redemption, West Bend, Iowa.

WEST BEND—Grotto of the Redemption is the largest grotto in the world and was fashioned out of stone by the Rev. Paul Matthias Dobberstein. More than 100,000 people each year visit this hand-made creation which actually is a composite of nine separate Grottos: Garden of Eden, Stable of Bethlehem, Home of Nazareth, The Trinity, Ten Commandments, Gethsemane, Stations of the Cross, Jesus Laid to Rest, and The Resurrection. Father Dobberstein came to West Bend in 1897 and spent 42 years building the grottos, developing intricate patterns out of stone, mortar, crystals, agates, petrified wood and materials from every one of the United States and every foreign country. There is a stone from the South Pole and a 300 pound amethyst, second largest in the world, from South America. The grottos have an estimated geological value in excess of $2 million.

KANSAS

ATCHISON—St. Benedict's Abbey Church is a monument to the Benedictine Monks of the 1850's and 1860's whose saddle apostolate served the settlers through missionary circuits, and to the Benedictines of today who operate St. Benedict's College. In this impressive Abbey Church, the great marble Altar reigns alone in the main body of the church; in the crypt or basement are 29 altars for the more than 120 priest monks to offer daily Mass privately.

MOUND CITY—Shrine of Blessed Philippine Duchesne, Sacred Heart Church, houses a shrine depicting Blessed Philippine's missionary work among the Potawatomi Indians. Murals of famed Sugar Creek Mission adorn the walls.

SALINA—Cathedral of the Sacred Heart, downtown Salina, combines the classic architecture of ancient Greece and the functional forms of the Kansas grain elevator and silo. In this contemporary structure, Architect Edward J. Schulte has established a studied liturgical relationship to the columnar forms and curved surfaces of the grain elevators and silos that color the hinterland landscape of rural Kansas. A high crucifix and a great processional panel of sculpture keynote the front entrance. Noteworthy are the great crucifix of black ebony with a corpus of ivory, suspended over the main altar; the black marble altar and the powerful figure of the Assumption carved in stone and covered with gold leaf in the Lady Chapel.

WICHITA—Cathedral of the Immaculate Conception (known generally as St. Mary's Cathedral), Corner of Central and Broadway. Visitors who have seen the churches in Rome will appreciate the Roman Renaissance architecture of this cathedral. Two stately bell towers, each topped with a golden cross, and a huge center dome, also topped with a golden cross, modeled after one of the twin churches of the Piazza del Populo in Rome, dominate the skyline. The facade has massive columns of polished gray granite. The Main Altar is Romanesque, constructed of Carrara marble with the columns of Pavonazzo marble of a delicate cream color to harmonize with the alabaster-like whiteness of the altar.

KENTUCKY

BARDSTOWN—Visitors to St. Joseph's Proto-Cathedral, third Cathedral in the United States, marvel at the collection of oil paintings in this church built 1816-1819. On the walls of the nave are "The Annunciation" (Van Dyck), "St. Peter in Chains" (Van Dyck), "The Coronation" (Murillo), "St. John Baptist" (Van Dyck), "Flaying of St. Bartholomew" (Rubens), "The Winged St. Mark" (Van Dyck), "Descent of the Holy Ghost" (Van Dyck). These paintings were gifts to the Bishop of Bardstown, the Rt. Rev. Benedict Joseph Flaget, from King Louis Phillippe of France in 1824. History records that Bishop Flaget met Louis Phillippe (then the Duke of Orleans) and his two brothers when they were in exile in Havana, Cuba in 1798. Subsequently Louis Phillippe visited Bishop Flaget in Bardstown and received numerous courtesies. Twenty-five years later, after he was crowned King of the French, Louis dispatched a thank you note and the paintings to Bishop Flaget. Incidentally, Bishop Flaget paid the duties on the paintings and an Act of Congress in 1832 returned the duties to the Bishop. In 1950, the art collection was stolen from the Cathedral, recovered from the art underworld in Chicago by the FBI, and subsequently remounted in thief-proof frames.

COVINGTON—Cathedral Basilica of the Assumption was elevated to a Minor Basilica in 1953 by Pope Pius XII. Although the interior closely resembles St. Denis of Paris, the exterior follows the detail and Gothic style of Notre Dame of Paris. Paintings of Frank Duveneck comprise a group of three large Gothic panels on the east wall, and a fourth smaller panel on the west wall of the Blessed Sacrament Chapel. Mosaic Stations of the Cross reproduce in ceramic tile the renowned oil paintings by the Redemptorist Brother, Max Schmalzl. Upwards of 70,000 pieces of tile were used in each Station by craftsmen in Venice, Italy.

COVINGTON—Monte Casino Chapel, world's smallest church, 4 feet wide, 6 feet long, built in 1878 by a Benedictine Brother.

LOUISVILLE—Cathedral of the Assumption, 443 South 5th Street, is known for its paintings, including "Scene in the Life of St. Bernard", attributed to Rubens; "The Pieta," presented to Bishop Chabrat by Louis I, King of Bavaria in 1845; "St. Charles Borromeo in Prayer", given to Bishop Flaget by Ferdinand II, King of the Two Sicilies, in 1836.

THE BASILICA OF ST. LOUIS, King of France, New Orleans, is one of the most famous of U.S. churches. General Jackson attended the service to mark the U.S. victory over the British in 1815.

LOUISIANA

NEW ORLEANS—The Basilica of St. Louis, King of France, on Jackson Square, is one of New Orleans' historic landmarks. It received its royal rank of Minor Basilica from Pope Paul VI on December 9, 1964. When Louisiana and the Floridas were detached from the religious jurisdiction of Cuba in 1793, Don Luis de Panalver y Cardenas was named the first bishop. He arrived in state in July, 1795, and St. Louis was a parish church no longer but a Cathedral destined to survive as the oldest in what is now the United States. A further dignity came in 1850 when New Orleans became a Metropolitan See. In the midst of rebuilding the Cathedral, the roofers arranged the new slates on the lateral and central spires to form the double-barred archiespiscopal cross, as they are seen to this day. Probably no metropolitan Cathedral in the world bears so conspicuous a symbol of its high dignity. General Andrew Jackson is the most interesting non-ecclesiastical figure associated with the Cathedral. In a footnote in the Cathedral archives, inscribed there as casually as any of the other records of a half-million lives, we read: "On the eighth day of January, 1815, occurred the famous battle against the British Army from which the Americans emerged victorious . . ." This "famous battle" at the end of the War of 1812 is a military curiosity because, unknown to the belligerants, the peace treaty was already signed! In any event, Andrew Jackson had conquered the very army that had defeated Napoleon at Waterloo. When the triumphant hero led his men into the rescued city, he was the center of interest as, in refurbished uniform, he stood at attention during the solemn Te Deum celebrated in St. Louis Cathedral. Thus began an association between the future President and the Cathedral. Across the street, the Place d'Armes was renamed for him and a noble monument of Jackson on horseback erected. Especially noteworthy are an oil painting of St. Francis of Assisi attributed to Rubens; and an immense, semi-circular painting which fills the wall area above and behind the altar screen. Decorative, rather than devotional in treatment, this work depicts in heroic grouping the famous incident in the life of the Cathedral's patron saint, Louis IX of France, when he proclaimed the Seventh Crusade from the steps of another great Cathedral, Notre Dame in Paris. The work was probably inspired by Raphael's frescoes in the Stanze in the Vatican.

LOUISIANA

GRAND COUTEAU—Convent of the Sacred Heart, scene of a dramatic event in American Church history; the little known case of the apparitions of St. John Berchmans, and the miracle which led to his canonization. A simple, unadorned chapel marks the site of the miracle, recorded in 1866. The beneficiary of the miracle was Mary Wilson, novice of the Sacred Heart, who was restored to health after being given up by doctors. It is believed that Blessed John Berchmans appeared to the novice three times. Blessed Philippine Duchesne of the Religious of the Sacred Heart visited here in 1811 and 1829. In addition, Mother Cornelia Connelly, venerated foundress of the Society of the Holy Child Jesus, lived here after her conversion, and as a laywoman taught in the Convent of the Sacred Heart. The Convent is visited by thousands of pilgrims each year. Rev. C. J. McNaspy, well known editor, wrote: "Few spots in America have been so unpredictably involved in sacred history as a tiny town situated on what was, some 2000 years ago, the west bank of the Mississippi, not far from where it flows into the Gulf. It is called Grand Couteau, from its situation on a sloping ridge or "coteau"—not a lofty ridge, but a long one . . . Grand Coteau is reckoned a power house of spirituality. . ."

NEW ORLEANS—The Shrine of Our Lady of Prompt Succor, 2635 State Street, is the result of two promises made by Mother Saint Michel, an Ursuline nun. Mother Saint Michel arrived in New Orleans from France in 1810 bearing a statue of the Mother and Child and vowing to foster the devotion to Our Lady of Prompt Succor in the United States. After five years, she longed to establish a regular feast day for Our Lady under his new title. Her opportunity came when she promised Mary a Solemn Mass would be celebrated every year in her honor if she brought an American victory in the Battle of New Orleans on January 8, 1815. Although they were hopelessly outnumbered by crack English troops, the battle was miraculously a resounding victory for the American forces. The Mass was celebrated annually and, in 1851, Pope Pius IX proclaimed January 8 as the feast day of Our Lady of Prompt Succor. Today, Our Lady has a new chapel on the grounds of the Ursuline convent in New Orleans and Mother Saint Michel's statue is enthroned under a stone canopy.

NEW ORLEANS—In 1874, Father Peter Thevis, a German immigrant, promised to build a cemetery and chapel in honor of Saint Roch if the dreaded yellow fever plague spared his parishioners. Few died and those who lived built the chapel and cemetery to honor their new patron. On August 16 each year they flocked to the small Gothic chapel to kiss Saint Roch's relic and pray for his intercession in healing. Crutches, braces, shoes and plaster casts of hands and feet and faces are left behind by those on whom Saint Roch has worked his healing.

NEW ORLEANS—St. Anne's National Shrine, 2111 Ursuline Avenue, reproduces four shrines in one structure: Holy Stairway, (Rome); Complete representation of the Passion, Death and Resurrection of Our Lord (Jerusalem); Grotto and statue of the Immaculate Conception (Lourdes); Altar and statue, St. Ann and the Blessed Virgin (New Orleans). Summer solemn Novema, July 18-26; Solemn winter Novena, beginning the first Thursday of Lent.

ST. MARTINSVILLE—In the Catholic Church is the painting of St. Martin of Tours and the Beggar, (circa 1830) by Jean Francois Mouchet, son of the great 18th century artist, Francois Marie Mouchet. This work is over the main altar of the church. In the cemetery near the Catholic Church are the grave and monument of Evangeline, celebrated subject of Nathanial Hawthorne's poem "Evangeline," one of his greatest works.

MARYLAND

OLD TOWN—St. Francis Xavier Church, Newton Neck, St. Mary's County, is the oldest Catholic Church in continuous existence in Maryland, and in the American English speaking colonies. While the present church was built in 1766, its predecessor was a mission established in 1640, which puts St. Francis over the 300-year mark.

BALTIMORE—The Baltimore Co-Cathedral, Minor Basilica of the Assumption of the Blessed Virgin Mary, Northeast corner of Cathedral and Mulberry Streets, is the oldest cathedral in the United States and the Mother Church of Catholicism in the nation.

Its exterior dome is covered with gold leaf. Suspended from the arch above Our Lady's altar is the red hat bestowed upon Cardinal Gibbons by Pope Leo XIII, March 17, 1887. Custom demands it hang there until it crumbles to dust. The brightly colored umbrella and the elaborately cast bell on its long shaft are at either side of the sanctuary. These are the insignia of the Basilica. Hanging in the Basilica is the great canvas of Baron Charles de Steuben, painted for Louis XVIII, on a theme suggested by Archbishop Marechal and presented to the Basilica by that king. It pictures Louis XI, Saint and Knight of France, accompanied by his armor bearer, his Franciscan chaplain and one faithful retainer, burying one of his pestilence-stricken officers before the African city of Tunis in 1207. A painting of Baron Pierre Narcisse Guerin, commissioned by Louis XVIII and given the Basilica by his successor, Charles X, depicts the Blessed Mother holding the broken body of her Divine Son, which Joseph of Arimethea, Nicodemus and their helpers have just taken from the cross.

BALTIMORE—The Cathedral of Mary Our Queen, on a 25 acre site off the 5200 block of North Charles Street, is an immense church of contemporary design. Opened in 1959, the Cathedral of Mary Our Queen is already an international landmark. Two 234-foot towers flank the main entrance. A 20-foot statue of Christ the King is recessed into the large facade window which arches beneath the Crucifixion group. On either side twelve apostles stand guard. The view of the body of the church is breathtaking. The high altar with its 50-foot bronze baldachin, the shimmering rose window above it, the vibrant ceilings, the Stations of the Cross carved right into the arches, the graceful 72-foot arches themselves, the color-splashed walls, the gigantic stained-glass windows on either side, and the richly ornamented altars beneath them, are all fascinating.

WARWICK—Old Bohemia, or St. Francis Xavier Jesuit Church, one of the earliest Catholic institutions in America, was founded in 1704. The present church dates from 1792. Although Maryland did not grant religious freedom until 1776, the church grew. In 1745, an academy was founded. John Carroll, the first Catholic Bishop of the United States and the founder of Georgetown University in Washington, D.C., was one of its notable students.

MASSACHUSETTS

BOSTON—The Basilica of Our Lady of Perpetual Help, 1545 Tremont Street, was raised to its regal rank among churches of the world in 1954 by His Holiness Pius XII. The Basilica is known to many as the Mission Church. In this hallowed spot are two vases filled with crutches, canes and casts left by cripples who have walked away unaided, by the blind who have found their sight. The silver plaque on one pyramid of crutches was placed there in 1883 by Colonel P. T. Hanley of Civil War fame for the cure of his daughter, Grace. More cures followed at that time, and newspapers across the country hailed the Mission Church Shrine as "Lourdes in the Land of the Puritans." Under the altar of St. Joseph are the relics of St. Nazarius the Martyr, who marched under the bronze eagles of Caesar's legions. Father Joseph E. Manton, C. SS. R. writes: "When you realize that this Saint was baptized by St. Linus, the Pope who succeeded St. Peter, you feel you are looking through a window into history. You are looking at a link between Tremont Street and the Appian Way, between the Church of the subways and the Church of the Catacombs."

FALL RIVER—St. Anne's Church and Shrine, 818 Middle Street, was designed by Napoleon Bourassa of marble, granite and stained glass. The Upper Church is resplendent in blue marble; stained glass windows produced by Rault of Rennes, France, are one inch thick and speckled with air bubbles that refract the delicate hues of the spectrum. The Shrine of Saint Anne in the Lower Church for more than 65 years has been a mecca for pilgrims. Public Novena devotions are held Sundays and Tuesdays the year around.

IPSWICH—National Shrine of Our Lady of La Salette located in a cathedral of pines on Topsfield Road. Extensive grounds, the quiet seclusion of formal gardens and the wooded walks are the framework for a facsimile of the Apparition of Our Blessed Mother in France in 1846. Devotions each Sunday afternoon; during the summer, outdoor services at the Shrine; each weekday evening, Mass in the Shrine Church at 7:30 followed by the Novena Prayers in honor of Our Lady of La Salette.

ROXBURY—The Redemptorist mission church, 1545 Tremont Street possesses a copy of the picture of Our Lady of Perpetual Help, as do all other Redemptorist missions in the United States, that hangs in the Church of St. Alphonsus Ligouri in Rome. The copy was touched to the original and solemnly enthroned over the altar of this church on May 28, 1871. A procession of cures and favors has been continuous since then.

WORCESTER—St. Paul's Cathedral, 38 High Street. Designed both for beauty and endurance in the face of the rugged New England weather, the granite walls are both practical and pleasing to the eye. The granite tower, 145 feet high, contains a bell weighing 2500 pounds. St. Paul's liturgical art includes a beautiful crucifix, the corpus for which is the work of a Bavarian craftsman; painting of the Mater Purissima by Domenica Morelli (1816-1901) in the Shrine of Our Lady; Van Dyck's painting of the head of St. Paul; icon of the Virgin of Kazan; carved wood bas-relief of the Madonna and Child by Joerg Syrlin the younger, who became famous for his wood carvings in Ulm Cathedral in Germany at the beginning of the 16th century (this particular work, a single piece cut out of Linden wood, was carved between 1500 and 1505, probably as an altar piece. Its gold leaf and original colors are in an exceptionally good state of preservation.) At the head of the two side aisles and on the walls above the Stations of the Cross, are tapestries illustrating scenes from the Passion of Our Lord (these tapestries are from the 16th century and are good examples of the high period of Felism tapestry weaving.) Another interesting tapestry is of St. Peter bearing his cross, which hangs from the choir loft over the main aisle.

MICHIGAN

BLOOMFIELD HILLS—St. Hugo of the Hills, Opdyke and Hickory Grove Roads, is one of the 100 most notable buildings in America chosen by the American Institute of Architecture. This Norman Gothic Church, which seats only 350, was built of hand cut stone. The interior is monastically severe, lighted by a series of torches of peasant origin fixed in high niches on the side walls. A figure of Christ, carved in Oberammagau, highlights the sanctuary and High Altar. By direct Papal dispensation, St. Hugo's alone, of the thousands of Roman Catholic Churches in America, contains a crypt where members of the laity may be interred.

ST. HUGO OF THE HILLS, Bloomfield Hills, Mich., seats only 350, was built of hand-cut stone.

MICHIGAN

DETROIT—Ste. Anne de Detroit, 1000—19th Street, has special significance for students of secular and religious history. The Parish and the City of Detroit were both founded in 1701, and the development of Detroit and Michigan is part and parcel of the religious leadership of Ste. Anne. Ste. Anne's most famous spiritual leader was Father Gabriel Richard, 1767-1832. Father Richard was pioneer priest, patriot, founder of churches and schools, co-founder of the University of Michigan, only Catholic priest ever elected to the U.S. Congress, printer (he published Michigan's first newspaper). The crypt of Father Gabriel Richard's tomb, finished in tile like the great Bishop Laval's tomb at Laval University, Quebec City, is open via a special passageway from Nineteenth Street. Each year, the Grand Novena, preceding the Feast of Ste. Anne on July 26, draws huge crowds. Many come for other Novena devotions held each Tuesday at 7:30 p.m.

DETROIT—St. Aloysius Church, Washington Boulevard, adjoining the Chancery Building, in downtown Detroit. This "three churches in one" is an entirely new idea in ecclesiastical architecture. Probably unique in all the world, the arrangement of the seating allows worshippers on each of three separate floors to see and hear the priest officiating at the main altar. The original idea for this innovation came from the Cathedral in Milan, Italy. In the center of that Cathedral is a circular opening in the floor, some 20' in diameter, through which worshippers can see, in the crypt beneath, the miraculously preserved body of St. Charles Borromeo. The pastor of St. Aloysius, seeing this sight years ago, wondered why, if it is possible to look down into a basement level, would it not be possible to look up satisfactorily through an opening. Challenged by a site limitation of 72x100 feet for St. Aloysius, the pastor proposed the semi-circular church, built of granite and stone in a modernized version of Italian and French Romanesque archiecture. The Stations of the Cross are Carrara marble, each carved by Salvatore Roni, famous Italian sculptor. The mosaic dominating the sanctuary is considered one of the most beautiful examples of the art.

INDIAN RIVER—Indian River Catholic Shrine, Interstate Highway 75, one-half block west of M-68. Indian River Catholic Shrine in the rustic quiet of Burt Lake State Park is visited by thousands each year. It is hoped that the Shrine may be dedicated to the

Venerable Káteri Tekakwitha, whose cause is being investigated for Beatification, and who served as the inspiration for Calvary Hill. In the outdoor church is the world's largest crucifix: the Redwood Cross is 55 feet high and 22 feet wide. The bronze Corpus, sculptured by Marshall Fredericks, weights 7 tons. A first class relic of different Saints is embedded in each of the 28 steps of the Holy Stairs; the relics came from Rome, and the Shrine has a document of authenticity for each one. The Stations of the Cross are of hand carved white pine set on a field of redwood. They depict the Death March of Christ in a peaceful woodland setting leading to the Crucifix.

REDWOOD CROSS 55' high, 22' wide, dominates the outdoor church at Indian River Catholic Shrine, Indian River, Michigan.

THIS 210-FOOT SHRINE of the Missionaries, with a carillon of 61 bells, is rising on the Sault waterfront at Sault Ste. Marie, Michigan.

LANSING—Saint Mary Cathedral, 219 Seymour Avenue, is the only cathedral in the United States with a replica of Mt. Calvary in the Sanctuary.

MACKINAW CITY—Church of Ste. Anne de Michilimackinac, at entrance to Mackinac Bridge, longest suspension bridge in the world. St. Anne's Church, built around 1740 by the Jesuit missionaries, has been reconstructed on its original site within Fort Michilimackinac. The restoration is part of the Mackinac Island State Park Commission's program to reconstruct Fort Michilimackinac as it existed more than 200 years ago. Throughout the day, through a combination of sound and light, the marriage of a Michilimackinac couple in 1754 is recreated for visitors to the church.

MARQUETTE—St. Peter's Cathedral. The towers of St. Peter's Cathedral beckon travelers approaching Marquette from virtually every direction. The stained glass windows and a brilliant sanctuary, surmounted by a huge painting depicting Christ's naming Peter as the first head of the Church and giving Him the keys, merit special attention.

SAGINAW—St. Mary Cathedral, 615 Hoyt Avenue, was founded as a mission in 1853, as a parish in 1866, and as a Cathedral in 1838. A beautiful sanctuary.

SAULT STE. MARIE—Rising on the Sault waterfront where Michigan's permanent history began 300 years ago is a 2-story concrete structure in the form of a triple observation tower. This 210-foot high Shrine of the Missionaries consists of three, vertical rectangular-shaped columns topped by five viewing platforms placed at different levels so they may face all points of the compass. Site of the towers is Sault's Portage Avenue not far from the spot where Father Jacques Marquette built his first mission. The observation towers of the shrine are the first step in the complete replacement of the present St. Mary's Church. The 21-story towers will be the bell tower of the new St. Mary's, with a carillon of 61 bells.

ROYAL OAK—The Shrine of the Little Flower, Corner of Woodward Avenue and Twelve Mile Road (12 miles from downtown Detroit), was the parish church of the radio priest, Rev. Charles E. Coughlin. Rising on the outside is an immense tower, each face of which forms a Cross. This tower was erected on the spot where a cross was ignited when the Shrine was a shingle edifice. When the fiery cross, kindled by the hand of bigotry, burned within a few yards of the little shingled church, Father Coughlin said to himself: "I shall build a Cross which they shall not be able to burn!" He kept his promise. The Main Altar, set within a broad circular sanctuary, is the largest monolithic Altar in the United States. It is a solid block of white Carrara marble, 12 feet long, 4 feet wide, 3 feet high, and weighs 18 tons. Mass can be celebrated on either side. The material of the Altar is enhanced by carving: peacocks drinking from a fountain are an ancient symbol of life-everlasting; the lambs, wounded and victorious, are a symbol of the Risen Christ. The candlesticks of the Altar are made of ivory (eight elephant tusks were used) with massive bases of bronze brilliantly inlaid with champleve enamel. These same materials form the Crucifix suspended from the baldachin over the Altar, as well as the tabernacle which is built low so that the celebrant may be seen from any point of the church. The statuary, paintings, and the four side chapels (dedicated to St. Sebastian, St. Joseph, Blessed Sacrament, and Virgin Mary) are worthy of hours of study. Be sure to see the monumental Statue of Christ, the carved reredos, and the twelve foot painting of St. Cecelia over the main organ.

SHRINE OF THE LITTLE FLOWER, Royal Oak, Michig

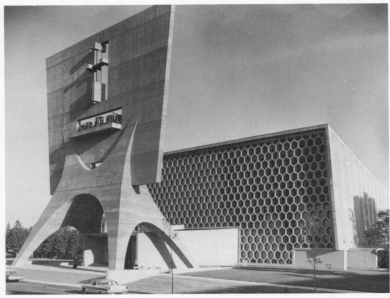

ST. JOHN'S CHURCH, campus of St. John's University, Collegeville, Minn.

MINNESOTA

COLLEGEVILLE—St. John's Church, campus of Saint John's University. Designed by Marcel Bruer, architect of the UNESCO Building in Paris, St. John's is strikingly modern. A dramatic bell banner at the entrance keynotes the philosophy of the entire church. The altar is in the center of the church, and around it, in a semicircle, are pews to accommodate 2,000. The side chapel of the Blessed Virgin contains a 12th century wood statue of the Madonna. The five bells in the bell tower were blessed in 1897 and were moved from the old church to the new tower in 1960. They strike quarter hours, the Angelus, and ring out before Sunday Mass and on other great occasions.

COOL SPRING, STEARNS COUNTY — Assumption Chapel is popularly known as the Grasshopper Chapel. The years 1876 and 1877 witnessed a scourge of grasshoppers. The farmers of Jacobs

Prairie and St. Nicholas parishes sought heavenly aid and vowed to build a chapel and dedicate it to the Mother of God under the title of her Assumption. The following day the grasshoppers disappeared. The chapel was built immediately but in 1894 a tornado literally tore it to shreds. One relic remained: the statue of the Virgin and Child which was carved by a farmer artist, J. Ambroziz. Today this statue occupies a place of honor over the altar in the restored granite Grasshopper Chapel.

MAGNUSSON ISLAND, LAKE OF THE WOODS — Fort Saint Charles, restored in honor of Father Jean Pierre Aulneau, S.J., "Minnesota's Forgotten Martyr." In 1736, Father Aulneau and 20 French companions, starting on a 1,500 mile trip by canoe to secure supplies for Fort St. Charles, were massacred by a band of Sioux Indians. The stockade and bastions of the fort have been rebuilt with cedar logs on the exact lines of the original fort. A chapel of concrete logs enshrines a granite memorial altar. Each year, in mid-July, the Fourth Degree Knights of Columbus of Minnesota sponsor an outdoor Mass at the Fort, thus preserving the memory of Father Aulneau as part of Minnesota's Catholic heritage.

MINNEAPOLIS—The Basilica of St. Mary of Minneapolis has the distinction of being the first church in the United States to be raised to the rank of a Minor Basilica by the Holy See. The honor came February 1, 1926. In anticipation of the honor, the name of the church had been legally changed in January, 1926 from the Pro-Cathedral of St. Mary to the Basilica of St. Mary, giving the parishioners a month's head start celebrating the regal honor. The Basilica is a striking example of Modern Renaissance architecture, and compares favorably in size, design and in the richness of its liturgical expression with the famous churches of the world. Especially noteworthy are the marble statues of the 12 apostles, replicas of the same group in the Basilica of St. John Lateran, Rome.

NEW ULM—Cathedral of the Holy Trinity, 605 N. State Street. The formal history of this cathedral dates only to January, 1958 when Holy Trinity became the Mother Church of the new diocese of New Ulm. As a church, rich in the historical tradition of Minnesota, and part of the pioneer leadership in the founding and early development of the city of New Ulm, Holy Trinity approaches the century mark. The contributions of its pastors and its congregations to the cultural, educational and spiritual life of Minnesota and to the United States, are etched deeply in history. The beauty of the Cathedral today was born of the Indian massacre of 1862, the cyclone of 1871, the grasshopper plague from 1873-1876, and the tornado of 1876, to mention a few of the hard pages from the archives of the past.

ST. PAUL—Cathedral of St. Paul, 239 Selby Avenue, is one of the largest church edifices in North America. Built of granite from St. Cloud quarries, the Cathedral is 307.5 feet high, 381 feet long and 216 feet wide. It seats 4,000. The majestic dome marks the architecture as Classical Renaissance. The Sanctuary and the main altar eloquently express richness, harmony and dignity. The seven stained glass windows are works of significance. Six columns of black and gold marble support the bronze masterwork Baldachin. Back of the Altar are seven bronze grilles commemorating seven episodes in the life of St. Paul. These brilliantly conceived and executed bronze works are internationally renowned. Three oil paintings hang in the Cathedral. On the walls of the rear piers are paintings of the "Crucifixion" by N. R. Brewer and "The Descent from the Cross" by Lehmann (1867) which was the altar piece in the Old Cathedral. "The Entombment" by Ribot of the XIX century French school hangs in the sanctuary above the minister's bench. It is one of the few original works of this artist in the United States. Four heroic mosaics (9'x15') from the famous Vatican studios are in the pendentives of the dome. Beneath the archway to the right of the pulpit are steps leading to the ambulatory which skirts the Cathedral apse. Along this passageway are grouped six chapels: Shrines of the Nations. They commemorate the preaching of the gospel by the national patron saints of the people who colonized St. Cloud and Minnesota. Main walls of the chapels are finished in Botticino marble; the marble background for each statue is from the country of the saint as are the cartouche above his head and the panel in front of the Altar. The statues are of Italian Trani marble. The figures of St. Anthony, patron of Italians; St. John the Baptist, patron of French Canadians; St. Boniface, patron of Germans; and St. Therese, patroness of all missionaries, are by E. H. Atkins. St. Patrick, patron of the Irish, was sculptured by Sidney D. Wollett; Saints Cyril and Methodius, apostles to the Slavic peoples are the work of Alban Polasek.

MISSISSIPPI

JACKSON—The Church of St. Peter the Apostle, 123 North West Road, was dedicated in 1846 and created the co-Cathedral of the diocese of Nathez-Jackson in 1957. The present church is the third one bearing the name of St. Peter. Two previous frame structures were destroyed, one by Union troops who invaded Jackson in 1863. The visitor to St. Peter's should take special note of its three altars of Carrara marble, and its 15 stained glass windows. (Carrara marble is the same marble used by Michelangelo in all his works.) The windows represent some of the finest examples of this art to be found anywhere. The twelve earlier windows were made in Munich and their workmanship, particularly with respect to perspective and color, cannot be equalled by modern artists. The two transept windows are reproductions of the paintings of the Immaculate Conception by Murillo and the Transfiguration by Raphael. However, in the Rose Window, "The Madonna of the Thumb," the stained glass artist took the liberty of having the Madonna face left instead of right as in the original painting by Sassoferrato.

NATCHEZ—St. Mary's Cathedral, Main and Union Streets, was begun in 1842, five years after the diocese of Mississippi was created with Natchez as its Cathedral City. Its first bishop, John Chanche, wrote to the king of France and received a Murillo copy of the "Assumption," and he wrote to the Duchess of Luca and received a marble altar. The cathedral bell was the gift of Prince Alexander Torloni of Rome in 1848. In the sanctuary is a prie-dieu presented to the second bishop of Natchez "From the Ladies of the Congregation, in thanks for the Bishop's liberation from military arrest, August 12, 1864." It was given to Bishop Elder after his release from prison for defying the Federal order to close his church after the city was taken during the Civil War.

MISSOURI

CONCEPTION — The Abbey Church of Conception Abbey was started in 1882 as the center of the monastery's liturgical life. The Holy Rule of St. Benedict that is the basis for life at Conception began about 1500 years ago in Italy when St. Benedict wrote his Holy Rule. Pope Pius XII raised the church to a Minor Basilica on September 14, 1940.

FLORISSANT—Old Ferdinand's Shrine, 416 W. Twelfth Street, was built in 1820 and is the oldest Catholic Church between the Mississippi River and the Rocky Mountains. Florissant's religious history is also the city's history. The frontier French village grew up around its parish church, old St. Ferdinand's Catholic Church, where Blessed Philippine Duchesne established the first novitiate of the Society of the Sacred Heart in the United States. Included among the present church furnishings are many pieces of religious and artistic significance including an 18th Century tabernacle which Mother Duchesne brought from France, as well as various altars dating from the early years, some of the original altar furniture, an altar figure, box pews, a sanctuary light, and two paintings, all dating from the 18th or early 19th century.

KANSAS CITY — Immaculate Conception Cathedral, 416 W. Twelfth Street. Visitors to this cathedral will see the famed Sanctuary Mosaic, which depicts in a contemporary manner the Immaculate Conception of the Blessed Virgin Mary. This Mosaic, 16x24 feet, was designed by Charlton Fortune. The Cross Tower and Dome, gold leafed, are a Kansas City landmark.

PERRYVILLE—The Shrine of Our Lady of the Miraculous Medal is within the Church of the Assumption of the Blessed Virgin Mary. The glory of the Shrine is the Carrara marble statue of Mary Immaculate as she is represented on the Miraculous Medal. Note the crystal and bronze candelabra; the painting, 18 feet in diameter in the center dome; the marble altar inlaid with mosaic; the beautiful stained glass windows; the marble urn with the image of Mary Immaculate in relief.

INTERIOR OF Conception Abbey Basilica, Conception, Mo., is beautified by paintings of scenes from the life of Christ.

MISSOURI

RHINELAND—Our Lady of Sorrows Shrine, Starkenburg Road, is actually the result of devotion to another statue of Our Lady. The second statue was known as the "White Lady" because of the ornamental white veil worn by the Virgin Mary. When a new church was built at Rhineland, the White Lady was considered too shabby and was placed in the attic and replaced by a new statue of Our Lady of Sorrows. In the third and present church, the White Lady once again has precedence. She is enthroned under the marble baldachin of the main altar and the statue of Our Lady of Sorrows stands in a side chapel.

SAINT CHARLES—Sacred Heart Academy was founded in 1818 by Mother Philippine Duchesne of the Religious of the Sacred Heart of Jesus. Thirty-four years later, after laboring in other Missouri cities and among the Kansas Indians, she returned to this city to die. A memorial chapel has been raised in Blessed Philippine's honor and the body of the **beata** is enshrined in a tomb of rosy marble below the main altar. At the shrine, the room in which she died is preserved. Her work table, a small chair she covered with rawhide and the brazier where she warmed her hands may be seen.

ST. LOUIS—Basilica of St. Louis, King of France (the Old Cathedral of St. Louis), Third and Walnut Streets. This historic church, consecrated in 1834, is now part of the Jefferson National Expansion Memorial. It stands 150 yards from the fabulous Gateway Arch, the 630 foot stainless steel arch that commemorates Thomas Jefferson, under whose presidency Louisiana was purchased, and the pioneers who broke open the American West and gave America claim to her natural boundaries. The Old Cathedral was once the Mother Church for a diocese almost as vast as the entire American West. On the main altar are four reliquaries which contain first class relics of many famous saints and two relics of the crib of Our Lord. In 1841, Pope Gregory XVI granted to the Old Cathedral, in perpetuity, the same indulgences previously reserved only for persons visiting the Seven Basilicas in Rome. Three paintings given the church by Louis XVIII remain in the Basilica. The church bell was cast in 1772 and contains 200 Spanish silver dollars. January 27, 1961, Pope John XXIII decreed Basilican status upon this church, previously known as the Church of St. Louis IX, King of France.

ST. LOUIS—St. Louis Cathedral, Lindell Boulevard. This is the outstanding church of the Americas done in the Byzantine style. The Byzantine signature is the huge central dome which dominates the interior as well as the exterior of the building. Crowned with a gleaming, gold-plated cross, the central dome of St. Louis Cathedral reaches upward beyond the height of a twenty-two story building. The lavish Mosaics within the Cathedral required more than one hundred million tiny pieces of glass, precious and semi-precious stones. This rare art form dates back more than 16 centuries and its application in St. Louis Cathedral is probably without equal anywhere.

MONTANA

ST. HELENA—Cathedral of St. Helena is a real gem in the Rockies. By night, the fifty-six stained glass windows are alive as a gigantic fire. By day, the Cathedral fills its promise as a renowned Church of breath-taking beauty. Its form is Decorated or Geometrical Gothic. Twin spires, rising 230 feet, are capped with gold-leafed crosses 12 feet high and six feet across. The stained glass windows are protected by half-inch plate glass. The interior is a symphony of light and colors: ruby red, French gray, charcoal and gold. Among the outstanding windows are St. Helena's in the North Transept depicting the story of the finding of the True Cross, and Emperor Constantine's window in the South Transept—Constantine, the son of St. Helena, preparing to do battle, sees the Cross of Christ in the sky surrounded with these words: "In this Sign Conquer." Another is the Rose Window with its Musician Angels of Fra Angelico; the Rose Window has 10 panels, each panel depicting an angel playing a musical instrument.

ST. IGNATIOUS—St. Ignatious Mission (founded 1854) the second mission established in Montana and the first established by the Jesuits in the Pacific Northwest, is the world-famous mission for the Flatheads, Kalispels, Kootenais and Pend 'dOreilles. Still standing is the church built in 1891, which houses one of the nation's prized art possessions: 68 paintings (frescoes) which illuminate and adorn the walls and ceilings. These works are by Brother Joseph Carignana.

NEBRASKA

BOYS TOWN—Dowd Memorial Chapel of the Immaculate Conception stands on the grounds of Boys Town on a grassy and tree-shaded plot. The exterior design of the chapel was inspired by the Gothic churches of rural England. Its dominating feature is a tower surmounted by a copper dome. The interior of the church

'HEDRAL OF St. Helena, St. Helena, Montana, known as the Gem of Rockies. Twin spires rise 230 feet, capped with gold-leaf crosses 12' ■, 6' across.

is blends of marble and oak furnishings. The stained glass windows in the transepts of the chapel are a reminder that sanctity was not confined to the Old World. They depict such saints as St. Rose of Lima, the first canonized saint of the new world, and St. Isaac Jogues, the North American Jesuit martyr. The theme of the facade window is appropriate for Boys Town and is expressed by the Scriptural text: "Suffer children to come to me, and forbid them not, for such is the Kingdom of God." In an alcove previously used as a baptistry stands the tomb of Father Flanagan, the founder of Boys Town.

GRAND ISLAND — St. Mary's Cathedral, Cedar and Division Streets, consecrated in 1928, was built in the French Gothic style; the cathedral features five Carrara marble altars and a Rose Window from Italy.

OMAHA—St. Cecilia's Cathedral, 701 North 40th Street. Its soaring nave and twin towers are landmarks on the outskirts of Omaha. The unique style of the Spanish Rennaissance was chosen for the cathedral because the first clergyman of any faith to visit Nebraska was a Spanish Franciscan friar. This style of architecture, as it appears in Spain and now in Omaha, has been described as "nobility without arrogance, majesty without ostentation." Above the altar hangs an awe-inspiring crucifix. The head of Christ is not bowed in suffering and grief but rather is raised heavenward pleading mercy for His executioners. Many statues of South American mahogany adorn the sanctuary. The Stations of the Cross which adorn the walls are the work of Albin Polasek. Along the side walls are the eight "Singing Windows" depicting the great liturgical hymns of the Church and the nine lower windows showing the patrons and founders of religious orders in the Archdiocese of Omaha.

NEW HAMPSHIRE

ENFIELD—Shrine of Our Lady of La Sallete, Route 4A, is a well known New England shrine. Reproduced on the New Hampshire hillside is the apparition of Mary on the Holy Mountain of La Sallete in the French Alps. Conducted by the Oblates of Our Lady of La Sallete, the shrine features a Way of the Cross that stretches for one quarter mile across the hillside and a Rosary made of 155 artificial roses which encircles the lake. Candlelight processions are held near the lake each evening.

COLEBROOK—Shrine of Our Lady of Grace, Route 3, one mile south of Colebrook, stands high in the White Mountains of New Hampshire. It is maintained by the Oblate Fathers of Mary Immaculate. The Shrine features an outdoor Way of the Cross sculptured from Quebec granite and Carrara marble. The Calvary group is life-size with a 14-foot Cross and a 6-foot Christus carved from a single block of marble. The fifteen mysteries of the Rosary are represented in granite. A giant replica of Bishop Sheen's World Mission Rosary with its decades of white, red, blue, yellow and green is also found at the shrine. Each bead of this Rosary is three feet in diameter and the entire Rosary is 130 feet long and 90 feet wide. A further memorial to the Rosary is the Family Rosary Lake and island at the shrine. On the island stands a series of six statues depicting a young family saying the Rosary before Our Lady of Lourdes. Stations of the Cross are said daily at 2 p.m.; the Rosary and Benediction at 3 p.m.

ONE OF THE MEMORIALS at the Shrine of Our Lady of Grace, Colebrook, N.H., is the Family Rosary Lake and Island.

NEW JERSEY

PRINCETON—Church of St. Paul, 214 Nassau Street, is a fine example of the American Gothic style. Constructed entirely of hand-cut granite, the church has in its tower three bronze bells cast in France. Its marble altar comes from the quarries and studios of Monreno Tedeschi in Pietrasanta, Italy.

STIRLING—Shrine of St. Joseph, 1050 Long Hill Road, atop a scenic hill in the Watchung Mountains. It was modestly begun by a few seminarians in 1924 who built a pedestal for the statue of their patron, St. Joseph. The shrine is maintained by the Missionary Servants of the Most Holy Trinity, a religious congregation of priests and brothers.

THE CHURCH OF RANCHOS de Taos in Northern New Mexico is considered the most beautiful Spanish church in the Southwest.

NEW MEXICO

CHIMAYO—El Santuario de Chimayo, Route 64, 24 miles north of Santa Fe, contains two shrines which the local Indians believe to be miraculous. They are the Shrine of Our Lord of Esquipulos and El Posito (little healing well.) The devotion to the six-foot Crucifix of Our Lord of Esquipulos was introduced from Guatemala. The Central American Indians believed the image to be miraculous and their faith in it has spread to the Indians of New Mexico. Many of the local Indians also believe that the mud which comes from a pit to the left of the altar may bring miraculous cures, and some Indians smear themselves with the mud. There is a room full of crutches, canes and braces left by persons who have been cured at El Posito. Interior painting and carving were done by Indians when the church was built in 1816. The ceiling structure is of a Spanish colonial style widely copied by modern architects in the southwest.

GALLUP — Sacred Heart Cathedral, 405 East Green Street, is located on the highest point in Gallup, and is the cathedral church for one of the largest dioceses in the United States (90,749 square miles). It is built entirely of brick in the Mediterranean Romanesque style. The focal point within the cathedral is a 14-foot cross which bears a 7-foot marble Corpus from Italy. The onyx altar below it was imported from Mexico. The four stained glass windows of the nave tell the history of the diocese of Gallup and the four transept windows depict the Church history of New Mexico.

RANCHOS DE TAOS—The old Mission of Saint Francis of Assisi holds the distinction of being the oldest unrestored church in the Southwest. Construction of the mission began in 1710. It is a magnificent specimen of Spanish missionary architecture and the art treasures approximate one half million dollars in value. The mystery painting, "The Shadow of the Cross," has baffled specialists for over 60 years. In daylight or in artificial light, it is a picture of Jesus standing barefoot on the banks of the Galilee. In darkness, however, the portrait becomes a self-illuminated shadow of a figure with a cross over the left shoulder. A halo can also be seen over the head and luminous clouds are visible in the background.

ISLETA — St. Augustine Church, Route 85, 15 miles south of Albuquerque, is reputed to be the oldest church in the United States **in continuous** use. Begun in 1613, it was found in ruins 80 years later and rebuilt in 1710. Its adobe walls are more than six feet thick. Old paintings and hand-carved statues are preserved in the sanctuary.

LAGUNA—St. Joseph's Church, Route 66, west of Albuquerque, is one of the most delightful missions of New Mexico. A wide band of bizarre red, yellow and green depicting primitive Indian designs runs around the wall of St. Joseph's church. The sanctuary ceiling is painted with colorful symbols of the sun, moon and stars. The walls are richly adorned with pictures of saints, among them a portrait of St. Joseph painted on elkskin.

SUMMIT—The Monastery of Our Lady of the Rosary, Junction of Morris and Springfield Avenues, was in 1921 the scene of the first outdoor public pilgrimage in honor of Our Lady of the Rosary in the United States. The Sisters of the Monastery has perpetual adoration of the Blessed Sacrament. The Monstrance is enshrined on an altar of Italian marble. Above the altar arches a Gothic baldachin supported by four columns of rare Siena marble with beautifully turned capitals. The Monastery possesses a replica of the Winding Sheet of Turin which is said to be the cloth in which Christ was wrapped for burial. The replica was made at the command of the Grand Duchess of Austria in 1624. The copy was afterwards laid upon the original Winding Sheet and, when it was removed, it was found that the Wound of the Side had become damp as though with blood and that this effusion had stained the replica. This circumstance has caused this replica to be held in great devotion.

SANTE FE—The Mission San Miguel dates from 1610. The mission paintings are two to three centuries old but the statuary is relatively modern having been carved in the Tyrolian Alps in the last fifty to seventy-five years. The San Jose bell is more than 600 years old and rang for three centuries in Andalusia, Spain before being brought to the New World in 1712 . Visitors may touch and ring the bell.

THE REREDOS, or altarpiece, of San Miguel Mission, Santa Fe, were restored in 1954-55; until then, the reredos were covered by a later, Victorian era altarpiece.

WITHOUT NAILS OR CENTER POLE, the circular staircase in the Chapel of Lorretto Academy, Santa Fe, N.M., has stood for 100 years.

SANTE FE—The Chapel of Loretto Academy of Our Lady of Light has a winding stairway connecting the chapel and the choir loft. The stairway makes two complete 360 degree turns although there is no supporting pole up the center. Some architects have said that, by all laws of gravity, it should have crashed to the floor the minute anyone stepped on it—yet it has been used daily for nearly 100 years. The stairway was built by an itinerant carpenter equipped with a hammer, a saw and a T-square **after** the chapel had been completed and the Sisters discovered the builders had forgotten to build in a stairway. Told by experts there was no room for a stairway, the Sisters prayed to St. Joseph. On the last day of the novena to St. Joseph, the itinerant carpenter appeared with a donkey and a tool chest. He completed the work in eight months and vanished. How one man curved the wood, secured a type of wood yet unidentified, installed the stairway and defied the basic law of gravity, constitute the inexplicable stairway.

NEW YORK

AURIESVILLE—National Shrine of the North American Martyrs, off the New York Thruway, exits 27 and 28, is on the site of the old Mohawk Village of Ossernenon. The shrine is dedicated to the three Jesuit martyrs of America and to their five Canadian counterparts. The shrine, built in 1885, has many reminders of their suffering at the hands of the Indians. The Hill of Torture, the Platform of Torture and the Hill of Prayer remain. The shrine also has a statue of Venerable Kateri Tekakwitha, who was born in the village of Ossernenon, and many other works of art including the statue of Notre Dame de Foy. The "Temple of 72 Doors" represents the 72 disciples of Christ; the 12 aisles represent the Twelve Apostles and the eight double doors represent the eight North American martyrs. Three of the doors face the United States, five face Canada.

TEMPLE OF 72 DOORS at National Shrine of the North American Martyrs, Auriesville, N.Y.

BROOKLYN—Our Lady of Lourdes Church, Aberdeen Street and Broadway. In the arch behind the altar stands a replica of Bernadette's Grotto in France. Behind the huge grotto is a painting of Lourdes as it appears today with its basilica, forest and Pyrenees Mountains in the background.

BUFFALO—Landmarks on the East side of Buffalo are the twin towers and cupola of St. Adalbert's Basilica on Stanislaus Street. This church traces its history to 1886 and to the zeal of a group of Polish emigrants. In 1907, Pope St. Pius adjoined the Church of St. Adalbert to St. Peter's in Rome, granting in perpetuity the privilege of enjoying all the indulgences and spirtual favors which the Vatican Basilica enjoys. The Sacristy of St. Adalbert's is extraordinarily impressive, as is the art work by Joseph Mazur. The Stations of the Cross are unique. Imported from Munich, Germany, they are partially carved of wood and partially hand-molded of papier-mache. The figures are mounted on wall plaques standing in relief and are three feet in height. Interesting are such details as the delicate carving of the hair strands, moles on some faces, the folds of the garments, veins and muscles and expressions of scorn and mockery of those who persecuted Jesus. The Stations are decorated in oil and gold leaf.

FONDA—The Kateri Tekakwitha Memorial, Route 4, ½ mile east of Fonda. The holy Indian maiden lived in this village from 1666-1677. She was baptized in a little bark chapel here in 1676. Today, the Franciscan chapel of St. Peter stands as a reminder of that first Catholic chapel in the Mohawk Valley. The Mohawk-Caughnawago Museum is also located at Fonda, serving as a repository of historical material pertaining to the Mohawk Valley Indians and Colonial settlers.

HAINES FALLS—Wayside Shrine of the Immaculate Conception is located in the heart of the Catskill Mountains. Mass is said daily and there are several novenas each week.

GRAYMOOR—Graymoor is a wayside shrine set against the background of fir and spruce trees on Route 9, 5 miles north of Peekskill. It has stood at the foot of Graymoor Mountain since 1945 beckoning tourists to the home of the Graymoor Fathers. Atop the mountain, in addition to the seminary, stand the Shrine and chapel of Our Lady of Atonement, the Graymoor madonna, and numerous smaller shrines and chapels. The tomb of Father Paul, the founder of the Graymoor Fathers, stands in the seminary quadrangle.

LACKAWANNA—The National Shrine of Our Lady of Victory, 780 Ridge Road, is one of the nation's first Minor Basilicas. Founded by Monsignor Nelson Henry Baker in 1920, the basilica features carved statuary from Italy, murals and windows from France and a variety of marbles from other countries. Its wealth of paintings and statuary reminds the visitor of the great European churches. The basilica dome is 251 feet in circumference, exceeded in the United States only by that of the Capitol Building in Washington, D.C. It is surmounted by a huge cross and both are illuminated at night. Father Baker, the "Padre of the Poor," is also the founder of Our Lady of Victory charity homes nearby the basilica. Free guided tours are conducted from 10 a.m. to 4 p.m. on weekdays and from 1 to 4 p.m. on Sundays.

MARYKNOLL—The home of the Catholic foreign mission society, founded in 1911, stands on a gentle slope, Maryknoll, near Ossining, on the banks of the Hudson River. Much of the architecture of the seminary has a Far Eastern flavor and there are three museums with treasures from the mission fields of Asia. In the seminary quadrangle, under its oriental canopy, stands the impressive statue of Our Lady of Maryknoll. The young missionaries kneel here to receive their mission crosses and lifetime assignments.

NEW YORK CITY—Church of St. Francis of Assisi, 135 West 31st Street, is the home of the National Shrine of St. Anthony, founded in 1930. Although the church is now buried in the heart of New York's business district, 26 Masses are said each Sunday to overflow crowds in the upper and lower churches. The crypt of the church holds a special charm. Mosaics, panelling of fumed oak, and works of bronze and wrought iron add touches of beauty.

NEW YORK CITY—The Church of Saint Paul the Apostle, 415 West 59th Street, is the church of the Paulist Fathers and contains the tomb of their founder, Father Isaac Hecker. The exterior of the church is 13th century old Gothic, but the interior has features of Byzantine architecture. Three of America's foremost nineteenth century artists, John La Farge, Augustus Saint-Gaudens, and Stanford White, were engaged to decorate the interior. A unique feature of the Church of Saint Paul the Apostle is its ceiling, colored in deep cerulian blue, which has the exact constellation of the midnight sky of January 25, 1885, the day of dedication of the church. The stained glass windows are of unusual beauty and other notable works are a mural of "The Crucifixion," one of the largest and most impressive religious paintings in the United States; a bas-relief of the "Conversion of Saint Paul" produced on 50 tons of stone and considered the largest single panel of its kind in the world; a painting of the "Martyrdom of Saint Paul."

NEW YORK CITY—St. Ann's Church, 110 East 12th Street, has been the site of the National Shrine of the Motherhood of St. Ann since 1929. Once the most fashionable of New York's churches, St. Ann's now stands as a reminder of times forgotten. The simple shrine of the Mother of the Blessed Virgin is still a leading place for pilgrimages in honor of St. Ann. The focal point of the shrine is an expressive Carrara marble statue set against a fluted drape of old rose at the immediate right of the sanctuary. The Saint looks down on her daughter, who is engrossed in the book she holds in her hands. Two relics of St. Ann are exposed for public veneration beneath and in front of the statue.

NEW YORK CITY—Saint Jean-Baptiste Church, Lexington Avenue at 76th Street, was founded in 1882 as the national church for French-Canadians. The shrine of St. Ann in the crypt is favored by the lame, blind and sick who come here to pray and light votive candles. Among the many notable visitors to the shrine was Babe Ruth who came to ask for help for an incurable throat cancer. Saint Jean-Baptiste Church has been granted an affiliation with the Church of St. John Lateran in Rome. The privilege of this affiliation brings with it many indulgences which can be obtained by a visit to this church as well as to the famous Mother Church of Christiandom in Rome.

HIGH ALTAR OF ST. PATRICK'S CATHEDRAL, Fifth Avenue, New York City, one of the best known of America's churches.

NEW YORK CITY—St. Patrick's Cathedral, Fifth Avenue at 50th Street, is almost lost in the complex of skyscrapers that surround it. Its French Gothic architecture makes it a leading tourist attraction in New York. In the year 1879, the "American Architect" Magazine wrote of the cathedral: "The scale is noble, the grouping and arrangement the real thing, the embodiment of long experience of the Middle Ages." St. Patrick's Cathedral has 17 altars but the main altar is the most memorable. Of the numerous side altars and shrines in the church, the new Lady Chapel makes a bright bower for the Virgin Mary as the light from the stained glass windows radiates on the statue and surrounding mosaics. October 4, 1966, His Holiness, Pope Paul VI became the first reigning Pope to visit the United States. After a 24-mile motorcade in New York City, he arrived at St. Patrick's Cathedral where more than 100,000 people crowded behind police barricades to see him. Inside the vast cathedral, 4,000 invited guests broke into spontaneous applause —a precedent shattering event in the normally hushed edifice—

when the white-clad Supreme Pontiff walked slowly down the main aisle to impart his blessing.

NEW YORK CITY—The Saint Cabrini Chapel of Mother Cabrini High School, 701 Fort Washington Avenue, contains the remains of the first American citizen to be canonized. Saint Frances Xavier Cabrini was the founder of the Missionary Sisters of the Sacred Heart. She was raised to sainthood in 1946 and her body was laid beneath the main altar of the chapel.

OGDENSBURG—St. Mary's Cathedral. The unique relationship between the episodes chosen from history and the scenes chosen from the Life of Our Lord makes the stained glass windows of St. Mary's Cathedral different from any other church in the world. A unified theme runs through every grouping of subjects. For example, beneath the principal medallion of Our Lord's birth are pictured other important birthdays: the first planting of the Cross of Christ on western shores by Christopher Columbus; the first penetration of a white man into territory of Upper New York when Champlain discovered the lake which bears his name; the first dedication of Ogdensburg to Christ when Father Picquet established Fort La Presentation on the site of the present city.

SYRACUSE—Cathedral of the Immaculate Conception, 259 East Onondago Street. As you enter through the narthex doors into the nave you are aware of a feeling of spaciousness and quiet dignity. The theme of the church is "To Christ Through Mary." All the Marian decorations point toward the focal point of Christ's High Atlar. On the south side of the Cathedral stands a marble baptismal font surrounded by a unique ceramic mosaic. 40,000 pieces, each one made individually and no two the same, make up this decorative work of art. It depicts the Biblical quotation: "Go, therefore, and make disciples of all nations, baptizing them in the name of the Father, and of the Son, and of the Holy Spirit."

YOUNGSTOWN—Our Lady of Fatima Shrine, Swan Road, five miles from Niagara Falls off Route 18, is described as an outdoor cathedral possessing all the architectural characteristics of a Roman style church. It is conducted by the Barnabite Fathers who have plans to erect a globe church with a statue of Our Lady surmounting it. The heart-shaped lake is surrounded by the world's largest outdoor Rosary.

NORTH DAKOTA

FARGO—Saint Mary's Cathedral, 679 Sixth Avenue North. The spire of this cathedral reaches 172 feet above the sidewalk. On the facade is a Carrara marble statue of the Immaculate Conception, and beautiful Roman style windows of Silican opalescent. The great white oak altar is especially noteworthy. Suspended behind the altar, and carried upward and over to form a canopy, is a large brocade and velvet tapestry in two shades of blue. Over the altar is a life size, hand-carved crucifix, the work of August Schmidt of Cologne, Germany. The crucifix, as well as the ambulatory grill flanking both sides of the main altar, the celebrant's chair, the bishop's throne, and the grill, are also Schmidt's work of a special white oak, imported from Germany. Aloysius Cardinal Muench's "red hat" or galero hangs in a specially constructed case in the vestibule of Saint Mary's. It is customary to hang the red hat over the main altar of the Cardinal's cathedral on the death of a cardinal. Cardinal Muench broke tradition and had his sent to Saint Mary's before his death.

CATHEDRAL OF THE
Holy Spirit,
Bismarck, North Dakota.

OHIO

BELLEVUE—The Shrine of the Sorrowful Mother, Route 2, was established in 1860 by Father Francis Brunner in a wooded area at Marywood, near Bellevue. At the entrance are statues of Mary, the Mother of Grace, and the Sacred Heart of Jesus, both Daprato statues of Biancoduro Carrara white marble. The grounds are dotted with statuary and Stations of unusual beauty.

CAREY—National Shrine of Our Lady of Consolation. Carey is located on U.S. 23, 57 miles south of Toledo and 80 miles north of Columbus. The image of Our Lady, Consoler of the Afflicted, was brought to Carey from the Mother Shrine in Luxembourg in 1875. From the earliest days of the Shrine, the Blessed Mother deigned to bestow favors on the afflicted who venerated Her in this sanctuary. It is the center of individual and group pilgrimages numbering scores of thousands annually. Evidences of cures and helps from disease and deformities are present at the Shrine. The basket of the man who was carried to the Shrine blind and a paralytic, remains as mute testimony of the love of Our Lady of Consolation. So do the many canes, crutches, trusses, braces, glasses, and other physical aids, which those fortunate enough to receive favors from Mary have discarded at the Shrine. The altar in the Shrine Park is a memorial to sons and daughters who gave their lives in World War II, and to all the deceased who were beloved by the friends of the Shrine. Both crowns are fashioned of diamonds and other gems set in gold and platinum contributed by pilgrims. Special Novena to Our Lady of Consolation, August 6-15.

CINCINNATI—Cathedral of St. Peter in Chains, 325 West Eighth Street, is one of the few churches in classical Greek style in the United States. It also is one of the most magnificent and imposing Cathedrals in North America. On the rear inside wall is a huge mosaic, made in Munich, Germany. Christ seated on the Throne of Heaven, gives the keys of the Kingdom to St. Peter. The panels in either lower corner depict the two times Peter was imprisoned in chains for preaching the Gospel of Christ, once in Jerusalem, and at the end of his life in Rome. The Latin inscription is from the Acts of the Apostles,'" . . . and Peter was kept in prison . . . bound with chains" a fact commemorated by the title of the Cathedral. Among the art treasures of the Cathedral is a genuine Cellini crucifix, the work of Benevenuto Cellini, one of history's greatest goldsmiths and sculptors, on display in the Archbishop's Chapel.

CATHEDRAL OF St. Peter in Chains, Cincinnati, Ohio, is one of the few churches in classical Greek style in the United States.

THE VAST INTERIOR of Holy Rosary Cathedral, Toledo, is enriched by the brilliant fresco on the Sanctuary dome.

EUCLID (Providence Heights)—The National Shrine of Our Lady of Lourdes, 21320 Euclid Avenue. Pilgrimage season and outdoor services: first Sunday in May through last Sunday in October. This shrine, established 25 years ago, is cared for by the Sisters of the Most Holy Trinity. Mary's Shrine, a replica of the famous Shrine of Lourdes, France, stands on a wooded hill overlooking busy Euclid Avenue. A rock from the grotto at Lourdes, France, is embedded in a stone beneath Mary's statue for the veneration of the faithful.

MARIA STEIN (South of Celina on Route 127)—The Chapel of the Sisters of the Precious Blood has a wealth of relics salvaged from churches being pillaged after the House of Piedmont took over the Papal States during Italian unification. The relics are now enshrined over the high altar of the chapel in exquisite reliquaries. Included are relics of the Cross, the life and death of Our Lord and His Mother as well as Apostles, martyrs, confessors, virgins and doctors of the Church.

TOLEDO—Cathedral of The Blessed Virgin Mary of The Holy Rosary, 2544 Parkwood. Few cathedrals approach the grandeur and majesty of this cathedral. It is the one Plateresque Cathedral in the world. Plateresque is an architectural style from the name of the goldsmith, Platerno, marked by delicacy of detail, reminiscent of engravings on precious plate. The vastness of the interior is enriched by paintings by Felix Lieftuchter, medieval stained glass windows by A. L. Pitassi, magnificent sculps by Frank Aretz. Especially noteworthy is the mammoth fresco on the Sanctuary dome, a Lieftuchter original panoramic spectacle of Church Triumphant, Church Militant and Church Suffering.

LY ROSARY CATHEDRAL is the one Plateresque Cathedral in the rld. Plateresque is an architectural style from the name of the gold-th, Platerno, marked by delicacy of detail.

OKLAHOMA

PRAGUE—National Shrine to the Infant Jesus of Prague (Intersection of Highways 62 and 99, about fifty miles east of Oklahoma City.) Novena and pilgrimage between the 17th day and the 25th day of each month. This shrine is a fitting memorial in the Free World, as the world-famous Shrine to the Infant Jesus in Prague, Czechoslovakia is still behind the Iron Curtain. On the grounds is a marble statue of the Infant standing on a marble world globe, showing an outline of the Western Hemisphere and of Europe. Two towns appear on the globe—Prague, Oklahoma and Prague, Czechoslovakia. Of special interest are a relic of the Manager of Bethlehem, and a relic of the True Cross.

TULSA—Holy Family Cathedral, 122 West Eighth Street, is known as the Tri Spired Gem. Deominating this edifice of Gothic architecture is the Cross standing 215 feet high surmounting the top point of the principal spire. Windows around the altar, in Mosaic expression, show the 12 Apostles.

OREGON

PORTLAND—Sanctuary of Our Sorrowful Mother, Sandy Boulevard at NE 85th Street. Lush green growth fostered by Portland's damp climate forms the setting for this sanctuary. Founded in 1924 by the Servite Order, the sanctuary covers 60 acres on two levels. Adorned with sunken gardens and overshadowed by a towering cliff, the lower terrace contains twenty acres alive with azaleas, camellias, roses and other shrubs and flowers. On this lower level stands the focal point of the Sanctuary—Our Lady's Grotto. Hewn out of a granite cliff wall that rises 150 feet, the grotto contains on altar surmounted by a white marble replica of the Pieta and two angels bearing torches. Standing just east of the Grotto is the Chapel of Mary Our Mother, a gem in modern-classical architecture. The beautiful murals of the Spanish artist Jose Rodrigo DeSoto adorn the chapel walls. Ascending to the upper level, on a cliffside elevator, the visitor may visit the Servite Monastery, the rustic chapel of St. Anne, St. Joseph's Grove, and St. Philip's Retreat. They may also follow the Way of the Cross or the Way of Sorrows. The Seven Sorrows of Mary are depicted with 34 elegant wood carvings winding along a sylvan path.

PENNSYLVANIA

ALTOONA—The Cathedral of the Blessed Sacrament, built in 1924, is of early Italian Renaissance architecture. Its dimensions exceed most churches in the United States with an over-all length of 244 feet and a width of 120 feet. Art works in the cathedral come from Italy, Belgium, and Spain. Its organ, the largest instrument on the North American Continent, was built by the old German firm of C. F. Steinmeyers and Company.

CONEWAGO — The Basilica of the Sacred Heart of Jesus was elevated to this rank on June 30, 1962, in recognition of the Basilica's history, its beautiful interior and wealth of art works. The Chapel of Relics contains relics of the True Cross and of four Jesuit martyrs: Ignatius, Aloysius, Francis Xavier and Peter Clever.

DOYLESTOWN—The National Shrine of Our Lady of Czestochowa near Doylestown bids to be one of the most magnificent in North America. Dedicated to the Blessed Mother, the Shrine covers 250 acres of rolling Bucks county countryside. The church seats 4,000 worshipers and although still in the process of completion, is in daily use. The Shrine includes the spectacular church, Monastery, a 46-acre cemetery. Among the original works of art are The Resurrection, an outdoor bronze, and The Holy Trinity mounted above the altar area in the upper church. Enshrined above the altar in an artistic rendering of the famed Black Madonna, the miraculous painting of Our Lady of Czestochowa.

HANOVER—Basilica of the Sacred Heart of Jesus, Route 4, received its rank of a Minor Basilica in 1962 from Pope John XXIII because of its history, beautiful interior and wealth of art works. Built in 1741 in the first distinctively Catholic settlement in Pennsylvania, the church was called Conewago Chapel during Colonial times. It is the oldest Catholic Church building in the United States built of stone and is antedated only by a few adobe Indian missions in the Southwest. The fresco of The Assumption was painted by Gebhart in 1845; the frescoes of the apse and transept ceilings and walls were done by Franz Stecher of Austria in 1851; and the "Apparition of the Sacred Heart" was the work of Costaggini in 1887. The Chapel of Relics within the basilica contains relics of the True Cross and of four Jesuit martyrs, Ignatius, Aloysius, Francis Xavier and Peter Clever.

STILL IN THE PROCESS of completion, the National Shrine of Our Lady of Czestochowa near Doylestown, Pa., bids to be one of the most magnificent in North America.

HARRISBURG — St. Patrick's Cathedral, Corner of State and Church Streets is characterized by Romanesque architecture. Notable art works in the church include 44 Munich stained glass windows including two transept windows depicting the Wedding Feast of Cana and St. Patrick Preaching Faith to the Kings of Ireland.

JOHNSTOWN — St. John Gualbert co-Cathedral, 117 Clinton Street, founded in 1896, was one of the first buildings in history to be built of structural steel. It is built in the Roman-Corinthian style of architecture. The main bell tower is 180 feet high and is an imitation of the Italian Campanile in St. Mark's Square, Venice. The smaller bell tower is 104 feet high and is a replica of the Choragic Monument of Lyscrates in Athens.

LATROBE—The Archabbey Basilica of St. Vincent de Paul at St. Vincent College received its Basilican status on August 22, 1955. Of major interest is the main altar of wide, table-like design. Two base blocks each weigh 2½ tons, and the cross-slab or mensa weighs 10 tons. The cream colored base blocks are Botticino marble: the mensa, dark green with gold veining, is Verdi Scuro Fraye marble.

Dr. Leo Ravazzi, a native of Pietrosanto, executed the four sculptured panels on the base blocks. As one looks at the altar from the nave, the right block bears a carving of Moses sacrificing the Pascal Lamb, while the left one portrays the impending sacrifice of Isaac by Abraham. Two more panels face the monks' chair. On the right is the sacrfice of Melchisedech and on the left, the sacrifice of Cain and Abel.

LORETTO—Just off Route 22, 2 hours out of Pittsburgh, nine shrines are nestled in the hills of the Allegheny Mountains. One of the principal shrines is the Prince Gallitzin Chapel House erected in 1832 by Father Demetrius A. Gallitzin, a Prince of the Court of Russia who renounced nobility for the life of a missionary. Father Gallitzin's tomb is located at Loretto.

The Shrine of Our Lady of the Alleghenies stands with an aura of keeping the mountains holy. The modern statue was done by a Religious Sister of Mercy. The face of Our Lady has features of the Mongoloid, Negroid and Caucasian races, a "Queen of Mankind."

Our Blessed Mother is honored under two more of her titles at

Loretto, too. There is an exact replica of the shrine at Lourdes, France, and an American version of the Portugese Shrine of Our Lady of Fatima.

The visitor to Loretto may also stop in the Church of St. Michael, St. Francis College, the Carmelite Monastery of St. Therese and Our Lady of Loretto Seminary, to complete the tour of nine shrines.

PHILADELPHIA—Cathedral of Saints Peter and Paul, 1723 Race Street. The green copper dome is visible throughout the center of Philadelphia. Built in 1846-64 in the Roman-Corinthian style, the church has an interior inspired by the Spanish cathedrals. It features Venetian glass mosaics and oil paintings done by Joseph Costaggini and Arthur Thomas. Two of the eight memorial chapels in the Cathedral are of special interest. The Archbishop Ryan Memorial Chapel is of the Celtic-Renaissance style with a nine foot Celtic cross surmounting the altar. The Holy Souls Chapel altar is modelled after the Blessed Sacrament altar in St. Peter's in Rome.

PHILADELPHIA—(Germantown)—Mary's Central Shrine of the Miraculous Medal is located in St. Vincent's Seminary, 55 E. Chelten Avenue, home of the Perpetual Novena of the Miraculous Medal. Since 1930, the novenas have been attended by more than 15,000 people each Monday. An astounding number of favors are granted as a result of these prayers. The statue of Our Lady of the Miraculous Medal is declared by artists and sculptors to be the most perfect of its kind in the United States and probably second to none in the world.

PHILADELPHIA—Saint Mary's, 252 S. 4th Street. In 1763, thirteen years before the signing of the Declaration of Independence, Old Saint Mary's was built on part of the burial ground of St. Joseph's Church. July 4, 1779, members of the Continental Congress gathered at Saint Mary's for the first public religious commemoration of the signing of the Declaration of Independence. The victory over the British was celebrated here on November 4, 1781 by a Mass of Thanksgiving, with members of Congress in attendance. George Washington attended Saint Mary's at least twice, first on October 9, 1774 during the First Continental Congress, and again on May 27, 1787 while the Constitutional Convention was being held in Philadelphia.

The Crucifixion Window over the High Altar was developed in Innsbruck and installed in 1888. The "Pieta", carved by Alfred Boucher from one piece of marble, was set in place in 1891. The stained glass windows in the lower windows on the north and south sides are from Munich. The cemetery adjoining Saint Mary's is the resting place of Commodore John Barry, the Father of the U.S. Navy; General Stephen Moylan of George Washington's Staff; Thomas FitzSimons, a patriot who was a member of the Constitutional Convention. Now in its third century, Old Saint Mary's is a shrine dedicated to the patriotism of our forefathers and also continues as a parish church.

INTERIOR OF OLD ST. JOSEPH'S, 321 Willing's Alley, Philadelphia, founded in 1733, now a National Shrine by Act of Congress.

PHILADELPHIA—Shrine of the True Cross in St. Michael's Chapel, Red Lion and Knights Roads. Simply designed walls of black Westfield marble form an impressive background for this shrine. The tabernacle door on the side altar of Our Lady is a replica of an icon at the Iberian monastery of Mount Athos. The icon shows the head of the Blessed Virgin with a slight scar on the right cheek. The scar on the original was caused by a lance thrust by a Tartar invader. Another feature of the Chapel is the baptismal font cover portraying the Baptism of Christ by St. John. It is a bronze sculpture of unknown date, attributed to the Italian sculptor Bernini of the Rococo School of the 17th century.

PHILADELPHIA—St. Joseph's Church, Willings Alley near Fourth Street. On May 14, 1733, Fr. Joseph Greaton, S.J., founder of the Pennsylvania Mission, bought property on Walnut Street between 3rd and 4th Streets. Here he completed in 1734 a **public** church, St. Joseph's. (A public church, according to English law, was considered an edifice standing by itself and completely devoted to religious services. At that time all denominations of Christians in Philadelphia, except Catholics, had public churches.) July 25, 1734, the Lt. Governor of Pennsylvania called his Council into session. "He had no small concern that a house lately built in Walnut Street was set apart for the exercise of the Catholic religion; it is commonly called the Romish Chapel. The Governor wished to know if the toleration of that religion was contrary to the laws of England." July 31, 1734, the Governer and his Council found that Queen Anne had approved William Penn's law of **Liberty of Conscience** (1706) which contravened William the Third's law against the Catholics. Thus the case was settled and Catholics were allowed to use the edifice on Walnut Street as a **public** church. Hence, July 31, 1734 (the feast of St. Ignatius Loyola, the founder of the Jesuits) is a significant day in the annals of Pennsylvania because religious liberty was acknowledged de facto for everyone without exception.

That's why St. Joseph's Church is considered the cradle of religious liberty in Pennsylvania. The present St. Joseph's Church (erected in 1838 and consecrated February 11, 1839) was made a National Shrine when President Dwight D. Eisenhower signed the bill that had passed both houses of Congress September 14, 1959.

PITTSBURGH—St. Anthony's Chapel, 1700 Harpster Street, Troy Hill, was built in 1892. Stations of The Cross are done in the realistic life-size style popular among Germans at the end of the 19th century. The large number of relics give this shrine special importance. All the Saints of the year are represented in this collection of more than 5,000 relics which also includes stones and various mementos from shrines in Italy and the Holy Land. The body of Saint Demetrius lies beneath the main altar of the Chapel. A gold case with the relics of all the saints mentioned in the Canon of the Mass serves as the altar stone and a splinter from the table of the Last Supper lies embedded in the altar.

RHODE ISLAND

MIDDLETOWN—St. Lucy's on West Main Road, established in 1950, was the first Catholic Church in the 200-year-old city of Middletown. The church and its rectory represent the extremes of Middletown's history as the rectory is one of the only two houses not burnd by the British during their occupation in 1777. It is a singular example of the pre-Revolutionary construction.

NASONVILLE—Indoor and outdoor shrines to the Little Flower of Jesus are located in this suburb of Providence. They are simple structures of ornamental stone and brick. Scarcely four months after the beatification of St. Therese in 1923, a series of extraordinary cures and favors focused attention on this humble shrine.

NEWPORT—The Navy hospital, Chapel-by-the-Sea is a landmark for all who sail in and out of Narragansett Bay. It is crowned with a colonial steeple and chimes dedicated to the memory of the USS Bennington dead in World War II.

SOUTH DAKOTA

BETHLEHEM—(Pierre) Towering Elk Creek Canyon on Interstate 30 is the site of a shrine created by the Benedictine monks amid 180 acres of fantastic scenery. In the cave, tourists travel the half-mile route to old Crystal Cave. Services are held at the Shrine twice each morning during the summer months, and during special religious days throughout the year. A fire is kept from the preceding easter and from this fire comes every course of flame at the Shrine.

TEXAS

AUSTIN—St. Mary's Cathedral, 203 East 10th Street. Built in the Gothic style, St. Mary's has stained glass windows from Munich. This church has the privilege of granting the famous Portuncela indulgence which was given to St. Francis of Assisi.

DALLAS—With its free standing arches, the interior of Christ the King Church, 8017 Preston Road, is reminiscent of European Cathedrals. The church's illumination consists of groups of three crowns, each progressively larger, suspended from the ceiling on heavy chains.

EL PASO—The three missions of the lower El Paso Valley are nearly one century older than the famed California missions and hold great historical and religious significance.

The **Mission de la Purisima,** Socorro, Route 80, 17 miles east of El Paso, was founded in 1683 and rebuilt in 1744. Its massive walls and unusual bellcote high above the main door are in the tradition of the austere mission style. The ceiling beams are a marvel of carving. The legend surrounding the statue of San Miguel says that the wagon bearing the statue to New Mexico from Mexico in 1838 bogged down in mud at the site of the present church. It was easily moved when the Indians took the statue out but then they were unable to replace the statue. They decided this was a sign that the saint wished a church built here in his honor. Later the statue was easily lifted into the niche prepared for it in the left transept.

MISSION OF CORPUS CHRISTI DE LA YSLETA (Body of Christ of the Island), 13 miles from El Paso, was the first of the Spanish missions in Texas. It was founded in 1681 and at that time stood on an island made by the channels of the Rio Grande. The church was rebuilt in 1744 and 1908 and the present church yard is the scene of ceremonial Indian dances. The mission farm of Ysleta has been in continuous operation since 1682. Its fruitful soil still bears a rich crop each year.

THE MISSION SAN ELIZARIO, 23 miles from El Paso, on a secondary road off Route 80, was originally established at Juarez in 1683 and reestablished on its present site in 1777. It was built to serve the garrison and government seat which was set up after the

Spanish victory of General Don Juan de Onate. San Elizario is excellently preserved and represents a type of architecture which supplanted the more austere styles of the two older missions of the valley.

SAN ANGELO—The modern Sacred Heart Cathedral of the diocese of Amarillo was consecrated in January, 1962. It is rich in symbolism which is carried out in the pews, the Communion rail and the stained glass windows. The only old furnishings of the cathedral are the three bells in the tower which were christened Mary, Angelo and Joseph in 1869.

SAN ANTONIO—St. Therese of Lisieux Shrine, North Zarxamora Street and Kentucky Avenue, the first church in the United States built as a shrine to the Little Flower of Jesus. San Antonio's shrine contains a Tomb Chapel which is a replica of the Tomb Chapel of St. Therese in Lisieux, France. Roses are the principal motif throughout the shrine; on the grillwork the work is so detailed each flower was hand-forged separately. Within the chapel stands a marble altar inlaid with mosaics and surmounted by a life-size, hand-carved image of the Little Flower. Five stained glass windows depict events in the Saint's life. Two other masterpieces in the shrine are "The Gloria" over the altar, made in Spain of hand-carved wood, and an oil painting of St. Therese. The painting was done by the sister of the saint, and was used in the canonization ceremonies in Rome.

SAN ANTONIO—San Fernando Cathedral, The Plaza. Built in 1738 by Canary Islanders with public donations and a 12,000 peso grant from the Spanish Crown. The present cathedral contains part of that old building and parts that are new. Its interior, in spite of renovation, has kept the spirit of Old Spain. The church stands on a plaza near the center of the city with fountains in the foreground.

SAN ANTONIO—The original Texas Longhorns were propagated and developed in the irrigated fields of the five missions surrounding the present city of San Antonio. However, the raising of fine cattle was not the only accomplishment of these missions and they are probably better known for their other activities and uses.

MISSION OF SAN ANTONIO DE VALERO, popularly known as the **Alamo,** is the most famous of the five missions. It is rich in both historic and religious significance. Founded in 1718 by Father Olivares, the Mission of San Antonio was secularized in 1793 and so technically was not Church property during the siege on March 6, 1836. However, it was not until 1883 that the property was sold to the State of Texas and before then it was the center of missionary activity. On March 6 each year, the Alamo once again becomes a church wherein solemn ceremonies are held to commemorate the sacrifice of the 187 men who died there to bring Texas to statehood.

MISSION SAN JOSE, Pyron Road off Highway 281, south of San Antonio, is the largest of the five San Antonio missions and is known as the "Queen of the Missions." Today it is a Texas State Park and marked as a National Historic Site. Founded in 1720 during the height of Spanish power in the New World, San Jose is considered the finest example in Texas of Spanish-colonial mission activity. The mission church was completed in 1778 and today visitors marvel at its unique style and ingenious construction. The Rose Window of the church is called the finest piece of Spanish-colonial ornamentation in the United States.

MISSION OF SAN FRANCISCO DE LA ESPADA (St. Francis of the Sword), Espada Road outside of San Antonio, was established on its present site in 1731. Visitors should take special note of its irrigation ditch and two century old aqueducts which still carry water.

MISSION CONCEPCION, Mission Road outside of San Antonio, had stood for over one hundred years before the Battle of Concepcion was fought there on October 8, 1835. In this battle, Col. Jim Bowie led the American forces in a defeat of the Mexican defenders of San Antonio. The battles of the Alamo and San Jacinto followed shortly and led to Texas statehood. The mission church at Concepcion is built in strong Renaissance style. Its two towers and dome are topped with graceful stone lanterns.

MISSION OF SAN JUAN, Mission Road outside of San Antonio, the last of the missions founded in 1731, was another link in the mission chain of the Southwest which was so important to the irrigation and cattle raising. Today's visitor will still see the remains of these two major mission activities at San Juan.

UTAH

SALT LAKE CITY—Cathedral of the Madeleine, 331 East South Temple Street, is one of the most beautiful churches in the United States. The Cathedral has mural paintings by Felix Lieftuchter and wood carvings by William Ross Company. The stained glass windows in the body of the Cathedral were made in Munich; the Stations of the Cross were painted by Robert S. Chase under the direction of Ralph Adams Cram. The warmth of color adds to the beauty and the devotional atmosphere of the Cathedral, and few churches surpass its beautiful interior.

VERMONT

ISLE LA MOTTE—St. Anne's Shrine, Route 129, on Lake Champlain. (Open daily from May 30 through October 15.) Conducted by the Edmundite Fathers, the shrine is on the site of Fort Saint Anne, the oldest settlement in Vermont and the site of the first Catholic Mass in the State. Relics of those historic days of 1666 are on display at the shrine. A small chapel was built there in 1893 and the St. Anne Shrine has sprung up around it.

WASHINGTON

SPOKANE—St. Charles Borremeo. Some visitors will find that St. Charles Borremeo shatters their traditional ideas of a church. It is one of the most modern in the West. Its basic structure is a thin-shell concrete arch called a hyperbolic-paraboloid. At the time of its completion in 1961, it was the largest unbalanced structure of its kind in the world. A tall, thin campanile rises 92 feet beside the church. There are no statues. Instead, stained glass has been used extensively. The "Last Supper" window and "sky" windows above the nave contain contemporary designs of the Passion of Christ. The Stations of the Cross are also represented in stained glass. The work was done by Gabriel Loire of Chartres, France.

TWO 175-FOOT TOWERS draw attention to St. James Cathedral, Seattle, Washington.

SEATTLE—St. James Cathedral, 804 9th Avenue, has two 175-foot towers which draw attention from the downtown district of Seattle and from the city's harbor. Dedicated in 1907, the cathedral is built in the 14th century Italian Renaissance style, is 220 feet long and 116 feet wide. In 1950, the interior was renovated by Harold Rambusch, one of the foremost church artists and decorators in the United States.

WEST VIRGINIA

WHEELING—St. Joseph's Cathedral, 13th and Eoff Streets, consecrated in 1926. The Cathedral is built according to the traditions of the Lombard Romanesque style of architecture. Its interior is decorated with marbles from Italy, Greece, Spain, and France. The stained glass windows are of particular interest. The western Rose Window is reminiscent of the limpid jewels of the Cathedral of Chartres. This is equally true of the two transept windows and the eight along the aisle.

WISCONSIN

DICKEYVILLE—Dickeyville Grotto of Religion and Patriotism, situated on the grounds of Holy Ghost Parish. The Grotto was conceived by Father Matthias Wernerus, Pastor of Holy Ghost Parish, 1918-1931. From the stones of the earth, from broken glass, precious gems, pottery, porcelain, Indian artifacts and concrete, Father Wernerus and his parishoners created a dazzling, sparkling Grotto surrounded by fifteen smaller grottos.

GREEN BAY—St. Francis Xavier Cathedral, corner Monroe and Doty, is pure Romanesque, enriched with fine glass, marble work, wood carvings, and paintings. In this cathedral is the Lady Chapel, Shrine of "Our Lady of Beauraing."

HUBERTUS—Our Lady of Holy Hill, national Shrine, Northwest of Milwaukee, Route 167. More than 100 years ago a priest stood on the ground of Holy Hill. He had a head full of dreams, a heart full of faith and empty pockets. Surveying the green hill-country, he said: "I feel sure . . . this hill . . . will become one of the most famed places in all this land; it will be consecrated and made holy . . . a place of pilgrimage and worship. Tens of thousands will come to do honor to the Virgin Mary and Her Son." This was the beginning of Holy Hill which goes back to the time of Father Marquette, the famous explorer. It received the name "Holy Hill" when the first cross was erected on its summit in the year 1858 — the cross may be seen in a glass case in the vestibule of the lower Church. Next came a rustic log cabin, then the present magnificent Shrine Church entrusted to the care of the Discalced Carmelite Friars. Holy Hill is a center of countless pilgrimages from virtually every part of the United States.

LA CROSSE—Cathedral of St. Joseph the Workman. The interior of St. Joseph's has the drama, richness, and dignity of the Cathedrals of Europe. Noteworthy are the Blessed Sacrament Chapel, the statuary, the stained glass windows lining the Epistle and Gospel side of the Cathedral which portray the history of the Church and Diocese of La Crosse.

MILWAUKEE—St. Josaphat's Church, 2333 S. 6th Street. Twenty-seven years after its dedication in 1901, St. Josaphat's Church was elevated to the rank of Minor Basilica by Pope Pius XI. If stone could talk, the stones used in the exterior construction of St. Josaphat's would probably tell an unusual story for they came from the old Chicago Post Office and Court House which had been razed to make way for a new building.

MILWAUKEE—St. John's Cathedral, 802 N. Jackson Street. The tower has pierced the Milwaukee skyline since 1847. Although there is much in the design to suggest the Spanish Renaissance, the church is a mixture of Roman and Greek architecture. In 1936 fire completely ravaged the interior of the cathedral. Notable of the new furnishings is the marble altar which stands beneath a hand-carved semi-baldachin and dome which rise to a height of 40 feet on eight stately marble pillars.

NEW FRANKEN—Our Lady of Good Help Chapel. In 1857, Our Blessed Mother reportedly appeared to a young Belgian immigrant in this northern Wisconsin community and instructed her "to gather the children in this wild country and teach them what they should know for salvation." The young girl and her father immediately erected a small log oratory on the site. Today, the fourth successor to this first church on the Green Bay Peninsula stands under the title of Our Lady of Good Help Chapel. It is a part of the pre-novitiate of the Sisters of Saint Francis. Although the apparition has never been officially verified by the Church, this shrine continues to attract numerous pilgrims each year, particularly on August 15.

DID YOU KNOW?

A GAME
TO PLAY

A GAME TO PLAY

* The world's largest outdoor crucifix (55 feet high and 22 feet wide) is at Indian River Catholic Shrine, Indian River, Michigan. The bronze Corpus was sculptered by Marshall Fredericks. How much does the Corpus weigh?

    Seven tons.

* Where is the Grasshopper Chapel and how was it named?

    Assumption Chapel, Cool Spring, Minnesota, one of America's noted chapels, is more popularly known as the Grasshopper Chapel.

    The years 1876 and 1877 witnessed a scourge of grasshoppers. The farmers of Jacobs Prairie and St. Nicholas parishes sought heavenly aid and vowed to build a chapel and dedicate it to the Mother of God under the title of Her Assumption. The following day the grasshoppers disappeared.

* Each bead of the Rosary is three feet in diameter and the entire Rosary is 130 feet long and 90 feet wide. Where is it?

    It's at the Shrine of Our Lady of Grace, high in the White Mountains of New Hampshire.

* Where is the oldest church in the U.S. in continuous use?

    Isleta, New Mexico, is the site of St. Augustine Church, begun in 1613, found almost in ruins 80 years later, rebuilt in 1710. Its adobe walls are more than six feet thick.

* On the site of the Old Mohawk Village of Ossernenon now stands the National Shrine of the North American Martyrs. Who were they?

    This shrine is dedicated to the three Jesuit martyrs of America and to their five Canadian counterparts. The Shrine has many reminders of their suffering at the hands of the Indians: the hill of torture, the platform of torture, and the hill of prayer.

* Why do thousands of tourists visit the Catholic church in St. Martinville, La?

> **Over the main altar of the church is the painting of St. Martin of Tours and the Beggar (circa 1830) by Jean Francois Mouchet, son of the great 18th century artist, Francois Marie Mouchet. And in the cemetery nearby the church are the grave and monument of Evangeline, celebrated subject of Nathanial Hawthorne's poem, "Evangeline," one of his greatest works.**

* Oldest Cathedral in the U.S. and mother church of Catholicism in this nation?

> **The Baltimore, Md. Co-Cathedral, Minor Basilica of the Assumption of the Blessed Virgin Mary. (Its great exterior dome is covered with gold leaf).**

* Where are the relics of St. Nazarius the Martyr, who marched under the bronze eagles of Caesar's legions?

> **Under the altar of St. Joseph in the Basilica of Our Lady of Perpetual Help, Boston. Father Joseph E. Manton, C. SS. R., wrote: "When you realize that this Saint was baptized by St. Linus, the Pope who succeeded St. Peter, you feel you are looking through a window into history . . ."**

* Joerg Syrlin the younger, famous for his wood carvings in Ulm Cathedral, Germany at the beginning of the 16th Century, created a carved wood bas-relief of the Madonna and Child. Where is it?

> **St. Paul's Cathedral, Worcester, Mass., noted for its liturgical art. Madonna and Child was carved from a single piece of linden wood, between 1500 and 1505, probably as an altar piece. Its gold leaf and original colors are in an exceptionally good state of preservation.**

* Father Gabriel Richard was a pioneer priest, patriot, founder of churches and schools, co-founder of The University of Michigan, and only Catholic priest ever elected to the U.S. Congress. Where is Father Richard's tomb?

> **At Ste. Anne de Detroit, Detroit, Michigan.**

A GAME TO PLAY

* Why is the National Shrine of Our Lady of Consolation in Carey, Ohio, the center of individual and group pilgrimages numbering scores of thousands annually?

> **Evidences of cures and helps from disease and deformities are present at the Shrine for all to see, including a basket in which a man, blind and paralytic, was carried to the Shrine.**

* The Sanctuary of Our Sorrowful Mother in Portland, Oregon, covers 60 acres on two levels. Half-a-million people visit this Sanctuary every year. How do they get from the lower level to the upper level to view the 34 elegant wood carvings depicting the Seven Sorrows of Mary?

> **They ride in an outdoor elevator which rises 150 feet up the side of a granite cliff wall.**

* It was in a dispute over the closing of a church in 1734 that religious liberty was acknowledged de facto for everyone without exception in the State of Pennsylvania. What church?

> **The church was St. Joseph's in Philadelphia, described as "the little Church in the Alley that was builded long ago." St. Joseph's was made a national Shrine by President Eisenhower in 1959 and was designated the "Cradle of Religious Liberty" in Pennsylvania.**

* What do Texas Longhorns have to do with the five famous missions in San Antonio?

> **The original Texas Longhorns were propagated and developed in the irrigated fields of the five missions. The most famous of the missions is the Mission of San Antonia de Valero, popularly known as the Alamo. On March 6, each year, the Alamo once again becomes a church with solemn ceremonies to commemorate the sacrifice of the 187 men who died there to bring Texas to statehood.**

* Where is the world's largest outdoor shrine honoring Mary, visited annually by several hundred thousand pilgrims?

National Shrine of Our Lady of the Snows, Belleville, Illinois.

* What is a Minor Basilica and how do you know you're in one?

Basilica is a title assigned to certain churches by the Holy Father because of their antiquity, dignity, historical importance or significance as centers of worship. Two of the symbols of the Basilica's royal rank are the Canopeum and the Basilica Bell. The Canopeum is a 14-foot umbrella made of twelve long strips of cloth alternating in yellow and scarlet colors. It is used to protect the Pope when he goes from one Basilica to another; it is always half open for instant use. The Basilica Bell is traceable to the custom of ringing a bell to announce the coming and leaving of the Holy Father when he visited a Basilica. The bell is not more than six inches in diameter at its lowest part and is mounted on an elaborate framework fixed on top of a banner pole.
"The Holy Father's Church" is another description of a Basilica.

* Father Matthias Dobberstein spent 42 years building the largest grotto in the world. He used stones, mortar, crystals, agates, petrified wood and materials from every one of the United States and every foreign country. There's a stone from the South Pole and a 300 lb. amethyst, second largest in the world, from South America. The grottos have an estimated geological value in excess of $2 million. Where is it?

West Bend, Iowa, is the home of the world's largest grotto, the Grotto of the Redemption, visited by scores of thousands each year.

A GAME TO PLAY

* Where is the famed desert church, built on a twin-pinnacled spur of red sandstone 250 feet high, jutting out of a 1,000 foot rock wall?

   It's the Chapel of the Holy Cross, Sedona, Arizona.

* Which Cathedral has exquisite murals by the Italian artist, L. Brustari?

   St. John the Baptist Cathedral, Fresno, California.

* The body of a Third Century Roman Virgin and martyr was removed from the Roman catacombs and enshrined in a U.S. Cathedral. Which Cathedral?

   St. Vibiana Cathedral, Los Angeles.

* March 19, St. Joseph's Day, marks the return of the Swallows to Mission San Juan Capistrano, Calif. When do they leave?

   October 23, every year.

* Where is the simple, unadorned chapel marking the site of the miracle, recorded in 1866, which led to the canonization of St. John Berchmans?

   Grand Couteau, Louisiana, site of the Convent of the Sacred Heart, scene of the dramatic event in American church history: the apparitions of St. John Berchmans to Mary Wilson, novice of the Sacred Heart, who was restored to health after being given up by doctors.

* On January 8, 1815, General Andrew Jackson led his American troops to victory over the British Army in the famous battle that was fought after the peace treaty was signed. Then what did the General do?

   He stood at attention during the solemn Te Deum celebrated in the Basilica of St. Louis, New Orleans. Across the street, the Place d'Armes was renamed for him and a noble monument of Jackson on horseback erected.

* Which church is so "modern" it has no statues?

> **St. Charles Borremeo, Spokane, Washington,
> whose basic structure is a thin-shell concrete arch
> called a hyperbolic - paraboloid. Replacing the
> statues is stained glass: a magnificent "Last
> Supper" window; Stations of the Cross are also
> represented in stained glass.**

* Half-a-million people each year visit Ave Maria Grotto where
125 miniatures of world famous shrines and religious centers are
displayed. Where is Ave Maria Grotto?

> **Cullman, Alabama.**

* Which cathedral has a great crucifix of black ebony with a
corpus of ivory suspended over the main altar of black marble?

> **Cathedral of the Sacred Heart, Salina, Kansas.**

* St. Joseph's Pro-Cathedral, Bardstown, Ky., has a priceless collection of 10 paintings attributed to Van Dyck, Van Eyke, Rubens,
Murillo. Who was the donor?

> **King Louis Philippe of France took refuge in the
> U.S., spent time in Bardstown, sent the paintings to
> St. Joseph's upon his return to France. Some years
> ago, the paintings were stolen, disappeared into the
> art underworld, were recovered by the F.B.I.
> They're now mounted on aluminum and firmly
> affixed to the walls of this church of classic col-
> onial architecture.**

* Where is the American "Notre Dame of Paris," elevated to the
honor of a Minor Basilica by Pope Pius XII, and which attracts
visitors from all parts of the U.S. and many foreign lands?

> **Covington, Ky., home of the Cathedral Basilica of
> the Assumption, whose beauty and dignity have
> spread its renown world-wide.**

A GAME TO PLAY

* The first canonized Saint who was an American citizen is memo-
ralized in a Shrine bearing her name near Denver, Colorado.
Who is the Saint?
   Mother Frances Xavier Cabrini.

* Huge stained glass windows (67'x13.5') are the work of Jean
Barillet of Paris in a famous Cathedral in Connecticut. Where
and which Cathedral?
   Cathedral of St. Joseph, Hartford.

* Largest Catholic Church in the U.S.?
   **National Shrine of the Immaculate Conception,
   Washington, D.C. On its outside walls are 137
   separate pieces of sculpture, a permanent museum
   of some of the best works of American artists.**

* First parish priest in the U.S.A.?
   **Father Lopez de Mendiza Grazales, Chaplain of
   the Fleet of Spanish Admiral Menedez de Aviles,
   who celebrated Mass September 8, 1565 in St.
   Augustine, Florida. This was 42 years before the
   English settled in Virginia, 55 years before the Pilgrims landed at Plymouth, 200 years before California's great Catholic mission, and two centuries
   before our American Declaration of Independence
   was signed.**

CATHEDRALS

IN THE

UNITED STATES

CATHEDRALS IN THE UNITED STATES

Albany (N.Y.) Immaculate Conception, Eagle St. (Madison Ave.-Jefferson St.)
Alexandria (La.) St. Francis Xavier, 628 Fourth St.
Allentown (Pa.) St. Catherine of Siena, 1825 Turner St.
Altoona-Johnstown (Pa.)
      Blessed Sacrament, 1215 - 13th St., (Altoona)
      St. John Gualbert (Johnstown Co-Cathedral), 117 Clinton St. (Johnstown)
Anchorage (Alaska) Holy Family Cathedral, P. O. Box 339.
Amarillo (Tex.) Sacred Heart, 819 Taylor St.
Atlanta (Ga.) Christ the King, 2699 Peachtree Rd., N.E.
Austin (Tex.) St. Mary, 201 E. 10th St.
Baker (Ore.) St. Francis de Sales, 2235 First St.
Baltimore (Md.)
      Mary, Our Queen, 5200 N. Charles St.
      Basilica of the Assumption of the Blessed Virgin Mary (Co-Cathedral)
          Cathedral and Mulberry Sts.
Baton Rouge (La.) St. Joseph, 423 Main St.
Beaumont (Tex.) St. Anthony, Res: 753 Archie St.
Belleville (Ill.) St. Peter, W. Harrison and S. 3rd St.
Bismarck (N.D.) Holy Spirit, 520 Raymond Ave.
Boise (Ida.) St. John the Evangelist, 8th and Hays Sts.
Boston (Mass.) Holy Cross, Washington and Union Park Sts.
Bridgeport (Conn.) St. Augustine, Rectory: 359 Washington Ave.
Brooklyn (N.Y.) St. James (Pro-Cathedral), Jay St. and Cathedral Pl.
Brownsville (Tex.) Immaculate Conception, Res.: 1218 E. Jefferson St.
Buffalo (N.Y.) St. Joseph, Delaware Ave. and W. Utica St.
Burlington (Vt.) Immaculate Conception, 98 Cherry St.
Camden (N.J.) Immaculate Conception, Broadway and Market St.
Charleston (S.C.) St. John the Baptist, 122 Broad St.
Cheyenne (Wyo) St. Mary, Res.: 2105 Capitol Ave.
Chicago (Ill.) Holy Name, N. State and Superior Sts.
Chicago (Ill.) Byzantine: St. Nicholas, 2238 W. Rice St.
Cincinnati (O) St. Peter in Chains, Plum and 8th Sts.
Cleveland (O.) St. John the Evangelist, E. 9th St.—Superior Ave., N.E.
Columbus (O.) St Joseph, E. Broad and N. 5th Sts.
Corpus Christi (Tex.) Corpus Christi, Rectory: 620 Lipan St.
Covington (Ky.) Basilica of the Assumption, Madison Ave.
Crookston (Minn.) Immaculate Conception, 204 N. Ash St.
Dallas-Foft Worth (Tex.)
      Sacred Heart, Ross Ave. and Pearl St. (Dallas)
      St. Patrick (Co-Cathedral), 1206 Throckmorton St. (Fort Worth)
Davenport (Ia.) Sacred Heart, Iowa and 10th Sts.
Denver (Colo.) Immaculate Conception, Colfax and Logan Sts.
Des Moines (Ia.) St. Ambrose, 607 High St.
Detroit (Mich.) Blessed Sacrament, Woodward and Belmont Aves.
Dodge City (Kans.) Sacred Heart, 901 Central Ave.
Dubuque (Ia.) St. Raphael, 231 Bluff St.
Duluth (Minn.) Holy Rosary, Wallace Ave. and E. 4th St.
El Paso (Tex.) St. Patrick, Arizona Ave. and Mesa St.
Erie (Pa.) St. Peter, 10th and Sassafras Sts.
Evansville (Ind.) Most Holy Trinity (Pro-Cathedral) Res.: 305 Court St.

Fairbanks (Alaska) Immaculate Conception (Pro-Cathedral) Res.: 115 N. Cushman St.
Fall River (Mass.) St. Mary of the Assumption, 407 Spring St.
Fargo (N.D.) St. Mary, 602 Broadway
Fort Wayne - South Bend (Ind.)
      Immaculate Conception, Calhoun and Jefferson Sts. (Fort Wayne)
      St. Matthew (South Bend Co-Cathedral) 1701 Miami St. (South Bend)
Gallup (N.M.) Sacred Heart, 405 E. Green
Galveston - Houston (Tex.)
      St. Mary, 2011 Ave. F. (Galveston)
      Sacred Heart (Houston Co-Cathedral) 1111 Pierce Ave. (Houston)
Gary (Ind.) Holy Angels, 640 Tyler St.
Grand Island (Nebr.) Nativity of the B.V.M., 207 S. Elm St.
Grand Rapids (Mich.) St. Andrew, 267 Sheldon Ave., S.E.
Great Falls (Mont.) St. Ann, Rectory: 715 3rd Ave. N.
Green Bay (Wisc.) St. Francis Xavier, Monroe and Doty Sts.
Greensburg (Pa.) Blessed Sacrament, 300 N. Main St.
Harrisburg (Pa.) St. Patrick, 212 State St.
Hartford, (Conn.) St. Joseph, 150 Farmington Ave.
Helena (Mont.) St. Helena, Lawrence and Warren Aves.
Honolulu (H.I.) Our Lady of Peace, 1184 Bishop St.
Indianapolis (Ind.) Sts. Peter and Paul, 14th and Meridian Sts.
Jefferson City (Mo.) St. Peter, 216 Broadway
Joliet (Ill.) St. Raymond, 614 North Raynor Blvd.
Juneau (Alaska) Nativity of the B.V.M., 5th and Gold Sts.
Kansas City (Kans.) St. Peter the Apostle, Rectory: 409 N. 15th St.
Kansas City - St. Joseph (Mo.)
      Immaculate Conception, Broadway and 11th St. (Kansas City)
      St. Joseph (St. Joseph Co-Cathedral) N. 10th and Isadore Sts. (St. Joseph)
La Crosse (Wisc.) St. Joseph the Workman, 530 Main St.
Lafayette (Ind.) St. Mary, 1205 Columbia St.
Lafayette (La.) St. John the Evangelist, Cathedral St.
Lansing, (Mich.) St. Mary, 227 Seymour St.
Lincoln (Nebr.) Cathedral of the Risen Christ Res: 3500 Sheridan Blvd.
Little Rock (Ark.) St. Andrew, 7th and Louisiana Sts.
Los Angeles (Calif.) St. Vibiana, Main and Second Sts.
Louisville (Ky.) Assumption Rectory: 443 S. 5th St.
Madison (Wis.) St. Raphael, Rectory: 222 W. Main St.
Manchester (N.H.) St. Joseph, 439 Pine St.
Marquette (Mich.) St. Peter, 301 Baraga Ave.
Miami (Fla.) St. Mary, 7506 N.W. 2nd Ave.
Milwaukee (Wis.) St. John, N. Jackson and E. Wells Sts.
Mobile - Birmingham (Ala.)
      Immaculate Conception (Minor Basilica), 400 Government St. (Mobile)
      St. Paul (Birmingham Co-Cathedral) Res: 2120 Third Ave., N. (Birmingham)
Monterey - Fresno (Calif.) St. John, 2800 Mariposa St. (Fresno)
Nashville (Tenn.) Incarnation, 2005 W. End Ave.
Natchez - Jackson (Miss.)
      Our Lady of Sorrows, 103 S. Union St. (Natchez)
      St. Peter (Jackson Co-Cathedral), 123 N. West St. (Jackson)
Newark (N.J.) Sacred Heart, 89 Ridge St.

CATHEDRALS IN THE UNITED STATES

New Orleans (La.) Cathedral (Basilica) of St. Louis, 615 Pere Antoine Alley
New Ulm (Minn.) Holy Trinity, 605 N. State St.
New York (N.Y.) St. Patrick, 5th Ave. (50th - 51st Sts.)
Norwich (Conn.) St. Patrick Rectory: 213 Broadway
Oakland (Calif.) St. Francis de Sales, Grove and 21st Sts.
Ogdensburg (N.Y.) St. Mary, 409 Hamilton St.
Oklahoma City and Tulsa (Okla.)
      Our Lady of Perpetual Help — Rectory: 3214 N. Lake Ave. (Oklahoma City)
      Holy Family (Tulsa Co-Cathedral) 122 W. 8th St., (Tulsa)
Omaha (Nebr.) St. Cecilia, 40th and Burt Sts.
Owensboro (Ky.) St. Stephen, 620 Locust St.
Passaic (N.J.) Greek: St. Michael, First St.
Paterson (N.J.) St. John the Baptist, Main and Grand Sts.
Peoria (Ill.) St. Mary, N. Madison Ave. and Green St.
Philadelphia (Pa) Sts. Peter and Paul, 18th St. and the Parkway
Philadelphia (Pa.) Byzantine: Immaculate Conception, 816 N. Franklin St.
Pittsburgh (Pa.) St. Paul, 5th Ave. and Craig St.
Pittsburgh (Pa.) Greek: St. John the Baptist, Homestead, Pa.
Portland (Me.) Immaculate Conception, 190 Cumberland Ave.
Portland (Ore.) Immaculate Conception, N.W. 18th Ave. and Couch Sts.
Providence (R.I.) Sts. Peter and Paul, Cathedral Sq.
Pueblo (Colo.) Sacred Heart, 1025 N. Grand St.
Raleigh (N.C.) Sacred Heart, N. McDowell and Hillsboro Sts.
Rapid City (S.D.) Our Lady of Perpetual Help — Res: 520 Walpole Blvd.
Reno (Nev.) St. Thomas Aquinas, Second and Chestnut Sts.
Richmond (Va.) Sacred Heart, N. Laurel St. and Floyd Ave.
Rochester (N.Y.) Sacred Heart, Flower City Park
Rockford (Ill.) St. James (Pro-Cathedral), 428 N. Second St.
Rockville Centre (N.Y.) St. Agnes, 29 Quealy Pl.
Sacramento (Calif.) Blessed Sacrament, 11th and K Sts.
Saginaw (Mich.) St. Mary, 605 Hoyt Ave.
St. Augustine (Fla.) St. Augustine, 40 Cathedral Pl.
St. Cloud (Minn.) St. Mary, 8th Ave. and First St., S.
St. Louis (Mo.) St. Louis, Lindell Blvd. and Newstead Ave.
St. Paul and Minneapolis (Minn.)
      St. Paul, Summit Ave. (St. Paul)
      Basilica of St. Mary (Co-Cathedral) —Res. 88 N. 17th St. (Minneapolis)
Salina (Kans.) Sacred Heart, 306 W. Iron Ave.
Salt Lake City (Ut.) The Madeleine, E. South Temple St.
San Angelo (Tex.) Sacred Heart, 19 S. Oakes St.
San Antonio (Tex.) San Fernando, 114 Military Plaza
San Diego (Calif.) St. Joseph, 3rd Ave. and Beech St.
San Francisco (Calif.) St. Mary (Assumption) (Burned, being rebuilt)
Santa Fe (N.M.) San Francisco de Asis, Cathedral Pl.
Santa Rosa (Calif.) St. Eugene, 2323 Montgomery Dr.
Savannah (Ga.) St. John the Baptist, Abercorn and Harris Sts.
Scranton (Pa.) St. Peter, Wyoming Ave. and Linden St.
Seattle (Wash.) St. James, 9th Ave. and Marion St.
Sioux City (Ia.) Epiphany, 10th and Douglas Sts.
Sioux Falls (S.D.) St. Joseph, 501 N. Duluth Ave.
Spokane (Wash.) Our Lady of Lourdes, 1103 W. Riverside Ave.

Springfield (Ill.) Immaculate Conception, 813 S. 6th St.
Springfield (Mass.) St. Michael, 240 State St.
Springfield - Cape Girardeau (Mo.)
    St. Agnes, Jefferson and Cherry (Springfield)
    St. Mary (Cape Girardeau Co-Cathedral) 629 Williams St. (Cape Girardeau)
Stamford (Conn.) Byzantine: St. Vladimir (Pro-Cathedral) Peveril Rd.
Steubenville (O.) Holy Name, 403 S. 5th St.
Stockton (Calif.) St. Mary of the Annunciation, 425 W. Magnolia St.
Superior (Wis.) Christ the King, 1115 Belknap St.
Syracuse (N.Y.) Immaculate Conception, 400 Montgomery St.
Toledo (O.) Blessed Virgin Mary of the Holy Rosary, Collingwood Blvd. & Islington St.
Trenton (N.J.) St. Mary, Warren and Bank Sts.
Tucson (Ariz.) St. Augustine, 180 S. Stone St.
Washington (D.C.) St. Matthew, Rhode Island Ave. (17th - 18th Sts., N.W.)
Wheeling (W. Va.) St. Joseph, Eoff and 13th Sts.
Wichita (Kans.) Immaculate Conception, 303 E. Central Ave.
Wilmington (Del.) St. Peter, 6th and West Sts.
Winona (Minn.) Sacred Heart, Main St. and Wabash Ave.
Worcester (Mass.) St. Paul, 38 High St.
Yakima (Wash.) St. Paul, S. 12th Ave. and W. Chestnut St.
Youngstown (O.) St. Columba, 150 W. Wood St.
Apostolic Exarchates:
    Melkites: Our Lady of the Annunciation, Boston, Mass.
    Maronites: St. Marion, Detroit, Mich.

CHRIST OF THE OZARKS, giant statue of Our Lord, seven stories high, with an armspread of 65 feet, overlooks Eureka Springs, Arkansas, from Magnetic Mountain. The statue was erected by the Elna M. Smith Foundation, and is dedicated to any lover of Christ regardless of his type of Christian faith.

TRAVEL NOTES

TRAVEL NOTES